THE APOSTLES' CREED

George M Philip

Christian Focus Publications

© George M Philip
ISBN 1 871 676 38 X
This edition published 1994
Reprinted 1997
Previously published in 1990
by
Christian Focus Publications Ltd
Geanies House, Fearn, Ross-shire,
IV20 1TW, Scotland, Great Britain

Printed and bound in Great Britain by
Cox & Wyman Ltd, Reading, Berkshire

Cover Design by Donna Macleod

Scripture versions used include:
Authorised Version (AV)
New International Version (NIV) © International Bible Society, and published by Hodder and Stoughton
Revised Standard Version (RSV) © Division of Christian Education by the National Council of the Churches of Christ in the United States of America.
J B Philip's Translation (JBP)

CONTENTS

Page

The Apostles' Creed

Foreword by Rev. Philip Hacking

THE APOSTLES' CREED

I believe in God the Father Almighty, Maker of heaven and earth;

And in Jesus Christ His only Son our Lord, Who was conceived by the Holy Ghost, Born of the Virgin Mary, Suffered under Pontius Pilate, Was crucified, dead and buried; He descended into hell; The third day He rose again from the dead; He ascended into heaven, And sitteth on the right hand of God the Father Almighty; From thence He shall come to judge the quick and the dead.

I believe in the Holy Ghost; The holy Catholic Church, The Communion of Saints; The Forgiveness of sins; The Resurrection of the body; And the Life everlasting.

AMEN

FOREWORD

The Apostles' Creed is common to all denominations. As an Anglican who was privileged to minister in Scotland for some years, I am delighted to recommend this series of sermons by George Philip on the basis of the Faith as contained in the Creed. It is my hope that many Anglicans who quite regularly repeat the Creed will read this book and find renewal and encouragement through its teaching. Quite often in Confirmation classes we take candidates through the Creed as the basis of our Faith. Very often after that stage in our Christian experience we tend to neglect further study. These sermons will help to renew our awareness of the meaning of these historic Christian clauses.

There is another value in these printed sermons. They come through, not only with the solidity of biblical teaching, but also with the warmth and passion of a preacher. There is a consistent message here for any who are searching for genuine biblical Christianity, to see if it is relevant to life and to make appropriate response. True evangelism is not whipping up people's emotions but daring to ask people to look at the facts of the faith. George Philip does that clearly and in a systematic way which the Creed encourages.

Over the centuries the Scottish church has majored on expository preaching and this is a sadly neglected feature of much church life today, of all denominations. These sermons, although based around the Creed, are essentially expositions of the Scripture which inspired the Creed. Indeed our church formularies remind us that we accept the Creed not because of its antiquity but because it is indeed firmly based on Scripture. Anyone studying these sermons will be led back with renewed confidence to the Bible and even more to the Lord of the Bible.

Philip Hacking

These studies are not, and never were, intended to be technical theological papers. They contain the substance of a series of sermons on the Apostles' Creed, preached to a Sunday evening congregation, the majority of whom were under thirty years of age, in order to meet the need for a clearer understanding of what we believe. They have been used in many places as the basis of instruction in enquirers' classes in preparation for membership of the church. If they are read in this way, perhaps in conjunction with the Shorter Catechism, they could prove to be the beginning of a desire for ever fuller understanding of 'the faith once delivered to the saints'. These sermons met a need when preached and when they first appeared in print. They have been fully revised and are sent forth as 'helps' to Christian understanding.

The Scripture quotations are from the Revised Standard Version unless otherwise indicated.

George M Philip

CHAPTER ONE

I BELIEVE IN GOD

In an age of confusion and uncertainty it is important that Christians should know what they believe. It is necessary also to have some framework, or systematic statement of basic doctrines, not least to provide a starting point for biblical evangelism when we seek to contact the many who are completely outside the church and who have little or no understanding of what Christianity is all about. The statements of the Apostles' Creed are an effective starting point.

For a variety of reasons there is a general impression that the Christian faith has been discredited and is no longer relevant to man's experience of life in the closing years of the twentieth century, this being the scientific, the nuclear, the space age. Many consider that the Christian faith is no longer intellectually tenable, and part of the explanation of this situation is that the Christian church has not taken the trouble, or has not had the courage, to declare in categorical and understandable language the fundamental facts of the faith. But there are certain things which *have* to be believed about God, about Jesus Christ, about ourselves and about salvation before we may call ourselves Christians. And if we are Christians we are under obligation to be ready to give some statement of and reason for the faith we hold (1 Peter 3:15). We must be prepared to state what Christians believe, in language people can understand and in terms that can correct the vague sentimentality prevalent in matters of religion. There is a 'faith once for all delivered to the saints', and it is for this we must contend (Jude 3). People have a right to challenge us about what we believe, and there are both opportunities and hazards the moment we begin to talk about God.

The sum total of some people's religion, including that of many who go to church regularly, is expressed in the words, 'I believe in God.' But what kind of God is He? This generally meets the response that it does not really matter what you believe about God so long as you are sincere. This is both facile and futile for you can be absolutely sincere and yet be totally and utterly wrong. That is a tragic situation, because the whole of your life is based on what you believe, not only for this life but for death and for the world that lies beyond it. If what you believe is wrong the consequences can be disastrous. For example, you can get up in the middle of the night, go to your medicine cupboard and in all sincerity take a bottle that you think will help you. But what if you make a mistake and it turns out to be poison? Do you say, 'It does not matter so long as you are sincere?' Of course it matters! Again some people talk of being afflicted with chronic indigestion, and they take their usual tablets unaware that what is wrong is a deep cancer that needs radical, surgical treatment.

Take the latter illustration into the spiritual realm, for sin too is a cancer. Of course it matters what we believe! Many people believe that all will eventually be saved and go to heaven, whereas in actual fact, it is made plain from beginning to end of Holy Scripture that there is a hell to be shunned as well as a heaven to be gained. Many a person goes right through life in heedless unbelief, an unbelief sometimes nurtured by the church he has been brought up in, because he has never been told from the pulpit that he has a soul that needs to be saved.

In a denominational magazine there was an article by a prominent lady scientist professing to be a Christian.

In answer to the question of what it means to be a Christian she replied, 'To accept the simple teaching of Jesus, to try and follow Him, and to try and teach it to your children; that is being a Christian.' Could anything be further from the truth than that? Trying-trying-trying! But the Christian gospel is not about trying, it is about trusting. We must come to an end of our trying, and that is the point at which we can become Christians. Salvation is *not* achieved by self-effort or self-discipline. We have to trust ourselves to what someone else has done for us.

> 'Upon a life I did not live,
> Upon a death I did not die,
> Another's life, Another's death,
> I stake my whole eternity' (Valpy).

The woman's statement was sub-Christian, even though the name of Jesus was used in it. If the essence of being a Christian is trying to follow the teachings of Jesus and teaching some of the children to do the same, then the cross of Jesus Christ was the biggest waste of time and the most hideous fiasco that this world has ever known. In fact, if there is nothing more to the Christian gospel than this trying to follow the teachings of Jesus, then Jesus Christ Himself is thereby discredited, because He made it absolutely plain that He was in the world to accomplish something for men that they could never do for themselves, and that was to accomplish salvation from sin by meeting its price and dying its death and suffering its wrath upon the cross under the judgment of God.

We are not going to try to prove the existence of God, nor are we going to give a series of arid lectures on theology or philosophy. The Bible itself does not give us in any one place a logically formulated theory or doctrine of God. It presents us instead with a real and living God, active in human history and personal experience, a God who stands over against men as the Judge by whom all men are examined. There is in Scripture no denial of what we would call philosophical consideration or scientific examination. By all means let the thinkers think and the scientists examine. Let them correlate their evidence and set it forth. We are not cowards. We are not afraid to face the facts. But what we have to deal with is God, the Christian's God, who has made Himself known.

I BELIEVE IN GOD

The Christian says, 'I believe in God,' but many people of other religions and of no religion say the same. We have not made much progress if we simply affirm that God exists and we believe it to be so. In fact, we could be quite radical and affirm that to say 'I believe in God' puts us on exactly the same level as the Devil! Read in the New Testament, the Epistle of James, that practical, down-to-earth, plain-speaking man:

> 'You believe that there is one God. Good! Even the demons believe that - and shudder' (James 2:19 NIV).

The demons go much further than many church members; they believe and actually tremble! They not only believe in God, they know He must be taken seriously. In a very real sense the Devil himself - Satan, Lucifer, call him what you will - is one of the most rigorous fundamentalists with regard to Christian doctrine. He believes it all. Scripture affirms that the demons believe and tremble, *but* they do not bow. They do not confess, because this confession that we believe in God is far more than simply giving intellectual assent to the fact of God, or to the facts of the gospel. There are many people who believe the facts who are not Christians. They believe, but, although they know the gospel is true, they will not allow the truth to lay its rightful claim to their souls and to their lives, to all they are and all they have. When we speak of believing in God, we are saying that, because we believe God is, and believe what He has said and what He has done, we commit ourselves in trust and obedience to Him. The demons do not do that, and many religious people do not do that either. A highly intelligent Honours student asked her minister the question, 'What do you do if you believe it all, but do not want to be a Christian?' The problem was not one of belief but submission and obedience to God.

We must go on from the statement 'I believe in God' to ask *what* we believe about Him, and there is quite a variety of current beliefs about God. Some people, who think they are religious, sum up the essence of their belief by saying, 'Well, what is for you won't go past you.' Their God is something akin to blind fate. There are other people who think of God as being a benevolent grandfather in a rocking-chair somewhere far away in heaven: a nice old man with white hair, maybe a beard, a twinkle in his eyes, who gives children a pat on the head, and turns a blind eye to anything that is not quite right. There are many people, including intelligent university people, who think of God in that kind of way. It gives them a nice, cosy feeling. There are others who think of God in the same way as they think of the man from the Insurance Company, the agent who calls periodically and who, if you keep your payments up, will see you through. This is why people in some denominations seldom come to church, because they are not really interested, but attend occasionally on a Communion Sunday. They feel this keeps their names

5

on the membership roll and the church will do the rest.

What kind of God do we believe in? If you associate with godless unbelieving people, as we should (it is not right that Christians should have no unconverted friends and acquaintances. How then are they to witness?) you soon find out what they think about God. For many people their home is their god; their career is their god; their children are their god. If you dig deep enough, and especially if you get them a little annoyed, you will find many a time that fundamentally their attitude is, 'I am my own god.' That is exactly why so many people have made utter shipwreck of life and of society.

The Bible asks a pertinent question when it says, 'Can man by searching find out God?' (Job 11:7 AV). The answer is, 'No,' but people disagree. They say that instead of going to church they go mountaineering or sailing, and claim that when they are up on the heights or out on the deep they can sense God. I, too, have sensed God on the face of the ocean, in storm, in calm, and in the dead of night. You *can* sense God like that! The Bible says so.

> 'For what can be known about God is plain to them, because God has shown it to them. Ever since the creation of the world His invisible nature, namely, His eternal power and deity, has been clearly perceived in the things that have been made. So they are without excuse: for although they knew God they did not honour Him as God or gave thanks to Him, but they became futile in their thinking and their senseless minds were darkened' (Romans 1:19-21).

Man's personality is so constituted that he can be aware of God, and sense God in creation. But what *kind* of God is this that you can sense sometimes in the aloneness of the hills or the sea? Get out on the wide ocean in a ship weighing thousands of tons and find yourself in a storm, lifted, tossed and swayed about, with the darkness enveloping you, and the sense of power in the mighty sea frightening you. Look up into the heavens, where sometimes you cannot see star or moon, and you may become aware of the might of God, the power and majesty of God, and even the terror of God. But you cannot tell what kind of God He really is, nor can you tell what God thinks of *you*. Here then is the crunch. It is not what we think about God that really matters, but what He thinks about us.

Can we tell what God is like and what He thinks? We can, but only because God Himself has spoken. There is a word from God that in its totality is the answer to the fundamental, constitutional hunger of the human heart: a heart that cannot escape from the fact that God is. This hunger, this longing, is a tremendous affirmation of the existence of God. Think for a moment of the surging twentieth century. Watch people, listen to them, and you will find that from the depth of their personalities (sometimes coherently expressed, sometimes not) there is a tremendous cry of hunger, as a whole generation looks for something to live for, something meaningful, something with purpose. A Russian novelist once wrote about a land in which there were no signposts because there was nowhere to go. That is the pointless, empty nihilistic world and life which many people have and are frightened by.

If we listen to many popular songs, whether the old ballads or 'chart-toppers' we can often sense this same wistfulness and searching. It is almost as if people are aware that life and reality are there somewhere but they cannot be found. Many older people (and some not so old) constantly look back to what they feel were happier days. It seems as if life has somehow passed them by.

Whether in the plaintive and often sentimental music and words of the past or in the raucous music and strident words of the present day, whether in traditional theatre or contemporary drama, there can be traced this aimless emptiness, a longing and a hope that something or someone will turn up to meet the crying hunger of the human heart. We are all at times aware of something we can describe as a longing we cannot understand but which is there even in our best moments. The hymn writer expresses it:

> 'Our hearts are pained, nor can they be
> At rest, till they find rest in Thee.' (Tersteegen)

Go back to what we learned in school, even though we may not have been very enthusiastic about poetry. This cry of hunger we speak of is nothing new. For William Wordsworth there was a time when everything had the glory and freshness of a dream, but then he says:

> 'It is not now as it hath been of yore,
> Turn wheresoe'er I may,
> By night or day,
> The things which I have seen I now can see no more'.

Another passage says:

> '...trailing clouds of glory do we come
> From God who is our home'.

He goes on to speak of the growing boy:

> 'And by the vision splendid
> Is on his way attended;
> At length the man perceives it die away,
> And fade into the light of common day'.

This is why many young people nowadays tend to make such a clamour. They are afraid that in two or three years' time they will be living lives as dull and boring as they see their elders living. They are frightened, and something within them says, 'Oh no, not that!' We find the same kind of thing in the poems of Alfred Lord Tennyson, in for example, 'Ulysses':

> 'I am part of all that I have met;
> Yet all experience is an arch wherethro'
> Gleams that untravelled world, whose margin fades
> For ever and for ever when I move.'

Many confess they know this eager stretching out for life and finding it so elusive. That poem goes on to speak of:

> 'This gray spirit yearning in desire,
> To follow knowledge like a sinking star,
> Beyond the utmost bound of human thought.'

Wordsworth, whom we quoted earlier, goes on:

> 'Whither has fled the visionary gleam?
> Where is it now, the glory and the dream?'

Little wonder he speaks in that same poem of:

> 'Hearing often-times,
> The still sad music of humanity.'

This same hunger of heart is found in the passage in Acts 17:16ff. It describes how in the great city of Athens, so proud of its achievements and reputation in the realms of art and culture, there stood an altar inscribed 'To the Unknown God.' Before Paul ever started on the journey that took him to Athens he heard the heart-cry of the man from Macedonia (Acts 16:9). From the background of Greek culture and Roman law there came the appeal to the missionary apostle of the Christian gospel, 'Come over and help us.'

The great God-shaped blank in our lives can be filled only by God Himself, in Christ. 'He has set eternity in the hearts of men' (Ecclesiastes 3:11 NIV) and our hearts can never be at rest, till we find rest in Him. Is there a word from God to meet this need? Yes. God has indeed spoken. God has spelled out His nature, His power and His love, gradually down the generations of Old Testament history as men have been able to bear it and have known their need of it. The record of that spelling out by God of man's need and the answer to that need is what we have in Holy Scripture. God revealed Himself ever-increasingly, until ultimately, in the fulness of the time, He spoke His final and conclusive word in Jesus Christ His only Son, His eternal Son, whom He sent into the world, not only to speak to men but to work for men.

This is the God Paul preached to the Athenians, saying as it were, 'the God for whom your heart hungers and gropes longingly, futilely, Him declare I unto you.' In that great sermon, Paul speaks of God as the God of creation, greater than all He has made, giving to all creatures life and breath and all things (Acts 17:22 ff). We can never be self-sufficient; we can never be independent; we can never be master of our own souls. We are dependent. And always the word comes from this God who stands over against us. 'The God in whose hand is your breath, and whose are all your ways, you have not honoured' (Daniel 5:23).

God is the God of creation, the God of history, the God who is the source of all nations and the governor of all destiny, upholding all things by the word of His power. This is the God we believe in. He is not a God who set the worlds in their place and then left them, but a God who is there ordering, moving, reigning and working His will through the generations of history. Why does this God take such an interest in what is going on in this tiny little planet of ours? We have it in Acts

17:26-27: that men might seek after Him, and find Him. What a spirit of seeking there is in the world today, but how little seeking for God!

God is not far away, for He has come right down to our experience and to our world. This is the wonder of God that He came down in His Son Jesus Christ to live and to die and to rise again for the salvation of men! All that God is, is seen in Jesus. All His love and all His power are seen in the cross of Jesus Christ, that cross which is the final and the absolute indictment of human sin. The cross is the proof that you and I are sinners. *There* is the assessment of what human sin is, and there in the cross is the declaration of the judgment of God upon sin. None of us will ever plumb the depths of that judgment. For all our time on earth and in eternity we shall ponder the mystery of the word from the cross,

'My God, My God, why hast Thou forsaken Me?' (Matthew 27:46).

That is the judgment of God upon sin. There, at the cross, the Bible says, 'God was in Christ reconciling the world to Himself' (2 Corinthians 5:19).

God has spoken and has made Himself known so that we are not left in any doubt as to what He is like. But what is man like? He is a sinner, and he knows it, although he denies it. He is a rebel and he must be told it, even though he does not want to listen. What is man like? Go back to the opening of the Bible and to the story of the Garden of Eden. It says God was walking and speaking there in the cool of the day, and what did man do when he became aware that God was near? He hid. Men nowadays hide in arguments, in theorising and philosophising. God spoke. The voice of God was heard saying, 'Adam, (man, woman) where art thou?' This is not the voice of a judge calling a rebellious criminal to judgment, it is the voice of a father calling for a prodigal child. Man, where are you? Woman, where are you in relation to God, and to Christ and to salvation, and to heaven, and to hope and to eternity? Where are you? Hear the voice of the Father seeking for the prodigal, and declare 'I believe in God.'

CHAPTER TWO

THE FATHER ALMIGHTY

With the clear objective of learning what God is like, and so learning what faith in God is and calls for, we consider the second statement of the Apostles' Creed which speaks of God the Father Almighty, Maker of heaven and earth. We will not seek to give a fully reasoned theological exposition of the Fatherhood of God, nor of the Doctrine of Creation; we will simply seek to understand the Doctrine of God in terms of bringing it to bear upon our life and our experience in terms of fact and witness.

The question we must ask is not 'Do you believe in God?' because that question is in some ways irrelevant. God is, whether people believe this or not. Still, even among those who say they do not believe there is evidence of a desire and a searching in the world these days for some stable ground of being and some coherent purpose in living which in itself is an expression of a desire for some kind of God, someone outside ourselves who will be some sort of guarantee or hope in respect of life. People may not understand who God is, or what God is, or where God is, or how to find Him; but constitutionally the whole of humanity instinctively declares, in a variety of different voices, that God, or at least something greater than themselves, is. Therefore, the question is not so much, 'Do you believe in God?' as 'What kind of God do you believe in?'

This is a question that we must address to men's minds to probe their consciences, because there is no denying that the conscience of mankind is troubled. There is ample evidence of this. There is a general feeling of unease, but it is a feeling that is too often suppressed and denied coherent expression by people who crowd their lives with every possible thing so that they will not have to face up to it. That is why some people must be out every night of the week, and why some people switch on the radio or television the moment they get out of bed, so that there will be noise and pre-occupation from the very moment they are awake. The one thing they will not endure is silence, because in that silence they might become aware of this nagging feeling of dis-ease in their minds, and deep down in their spirits. It is a feeling that is often repressed, pushed down into the subconscious, as men and women try to pretend that it is not there, but all they succeed in doing is to cause this uneasiness of spirit to express itself in a different guise, such as rebellion or cynicism.

What exactly is this feeling? It is a feeling of uncertainty, though people do not like admitting to that. They like to assume that all is well, and even when you speak to them about God they hurriedly insist that they have no worries in that area. Yet there is a deep feeling of uncertainty in the minds, hearts and consciences of countless numbers of people, a feeling which at times becomes a sense of guilt. People are not quite sure why they feel guilty, or what they have done to feel guilty, but somehow or other there is this strange feeling of disturbance. You can sense it sometimes at a funeral service where a company of people are gathered - family, friends, neighbours and associates - and they are together because someone has died. The minister reads from the Bible and speaks in prayer regarding life, death, eternity, judgment and the need for the salvation of souls. Without necessarily wanting it, people are made aware of God and the reality of death and the shortness and uncertainty of life. Many will not be at ease, for subjects like these are not ones they like to think about.

They do not know what to do. They shuffle their feet. They try to look away and they try not to listen. Is it a sense of guilt? Without question it is a feeling of uncertainty, and they do not like it.

It is not hard to explain why people are like that. They know that God is, but they are not sure what God is like. They are not sure how they stand with God nor are they sure how to go about finding how they stand with Him. Into situations like these Christians are sent with the message of the gospel, which has no doubt about it, declaring to men and women living in uncertainty and suppressed apprehension that we believe in God the Father Almighty, Maker of heaven and earth. That statement speaks of God as a real God, a personal God, a God who has the heart of a father and who has the power of a creator. Such is the tremendous affirmation that we have to make in the context of our modern civilisation, which is so arrogantly sure of its knowledge and skills and yet at the same time is so desperately unsure of itself.

I believe in God the Father Almighty, Maker of heaven and earth. That is a dogmatic statement, an affirmation without qualification but a description that is comprehensive. Yet when it is made we find it is often resented and refused on the grounds that we must do away with dogma. People say that mankind has come of age and it is no longer necessary or desirable to have the church laying down the law as to what we should believe. Away with dogma! Away with statements of what is to be believed about God, church, life, death, the world and eternity! The demand nowadays in many colleges and seminaries is for what is called 'open-ended theology'. But something open at both ends is very soon empty! Do men mean that we must have a theology, a word about God, that is adjustable and changeable, so that, whatever

15

your inclination or situation, whatever the changing fashions and philosophies of the age, you just re-write the doctrine of God? God is infinite, eternal, unchangeable and unchanging. Open-ended theology is not the theology of the Word of God.

Without doubt, in all generations, the need of the world, the need of the social community and the working place and the need of every home is for an affirmative word about God. It may not be the *demand* but it is the *need*, whether it is recognised or not. There are so many 'voices' proclaiming so many 'messages', all purporting to be the truth people need to solve the world's problems, that people are confused, and perhaps the younger generation is more confused than most. Social and political philosophies are proclaimed and peddled with almost 'messianic' fervour; 'religions' (especially eastern religions) and techniques of meditation all make their claim to be the answer to human need. If ever there was a time calling for a sure and clear word from God about God, it is now. But at the same time, we find many people abandoning churches because so much of contemporary preaching lacks both biblical content and conviction. In fact, some sermons (and I refer to specific instances) never mention God or Jesus Christ. People are left wondering if there is anything definite at all to believe about God.

Some years ago (many will not recall the time) there was a popular record on 'Top of the Pops' with surprising words. They were virtually verbatim from Ecclesiastes 3:1-8 emphasising that there is a time for every purpose under heaven. I am not sure what significance the writers of the song gave to the words, or what the producers of the record understood by them or what the objective was in promoting the record. What do these words mean, 'A time to be born and a time to die, a time to love and a time to refrain, a time to get and a time to lose'? Is this passage from Ecclesiastes, as some would say, an affirmation of the over-ruling providence of God? Are these words meant to make us aware of an unseen governor - a controller of all we have and are, and of all the circumstances and developments of life? It says earlier in Ecclesiastes, 'Whatever my eyes saw, whatever my heart desired, that I gave it' (2:9-11). Is this then the testimony from human experience of a man who gave himself to everything that there was to do in life and found only vanity? Could it not be that this passage has been taken up by a younger generation as a complaint against the aimlessness and the futility of life? If this is the meaning that was attached to this popular record, then it was a cry from the heart of countless people for a God to make sense of the world and of personal experience. When I listened to the words and heard the repeated phrase, 'Turn, turn, turn,' a verse of the Bible came to mind. God, through the prophet Ezekiel, is speaking to the people who are adrift upon the sea of life, and He is calling to them, 'Turn ye, turn ye, why will ye die?' (Ezekiel 33:11 AV).

Who then, is this God we are called to turn to in Jesus Christ? He is God the Father Almighty, Maker of heaven and earth. If we take the words 'Almighty Creator' we have a phrase that speaks of tremendous power that is almost frightening. If we take the word 'Father', we have a word which still speaks of authority, but speaks also of dependability and of personal, individual care. This God of power and care, this God of purpose and mercy is the God of the Christian message. This is the great and mighty and living God who is always pressing in upon men, reminding us all of Himself and convicting us of our sin, our rebellion and our judgment.

MAKER OF HEAVEN AND EARTH

When we speak of God as Maker of heaven and earth, almost instantly some scientists object, saying they reject the Christian doctrine of creation, and they bring forth all sorts of astonishing facts that are beyond the average mind to grasp. They lose us by the sheer dimension of measurements. They lay before us all their correlated statistics and formulated theories to explain the origin of matter, the world of creation. Of course we must always remember that the conflicting theories of the scientists (and there is by no means unanimity) are concerned with *how* the world was made. That is not the Christian concern. The Christian is concerned with *who* made the world and *why* the world was made. Therefore, the Christian is concerned, as he considers creation, not with the mechanics of the beginning but with the objectives of the Creator.

When we turn to the opening chapter of the Bible (and the Christian doctrine of creation is by no means confined to the Book of Genesis), we read, 'In the beginning, God...'. God spoke, and by the word of His mouth He called into being, out of nothing, all that we call matter, all the stuff, the substance of the created order of the universe. He spoke and it was done, and there was no difficulty in His doing it. When we speak of God as the Maker of heaven and earth, we are declaring that we have a world that is distinct from God, and yet always dependent on Him.

This doctrine is found throughout the whole of the Bible, and yet we never really find a full answer telling why God created the world. There was *no need* for Him to create. He lacked nothing. He was eternally sufficient in Himself. Why then did He create the world? We can only say that He chose to create. It was part of His purpose. It provided the theatre on whose stage He could demonstrate the glory of His grace and the wonder of His love. When we insist on demanding full explanations we need to remember that we have no right to require the Creator to explain. He does what He chooses to do and has every right to do so without reference to any mere creature. Read the great passage in Isaiah 40:12-26, 28, and link these sweeping statements with the words of the intellectual missionary statesman Paul in Romans 11:33-36. Who are we to demand detailed explanations from God concerning why and by what means He works His mighty works?

If we are to begin to understand the world in which we live we must lay aside our pride and see ourselves for what we really are: puny, limited, circumscribed, insufficient, utterly dependent; while God stands over against us in the majesty of His person, the almightiness of His power, and the sufficiency of His own heart and His own purpose. He chose to create and through that creation to reveal Himself, to make known what He could not reveal in any other way, the fulness of His love, and His redemption in Jesus Christ His Son. And when, in the fulness of time, creation has served the purpose for which it was brought into being, when God's saving plan of redemption is brought to its culmination, then all we mean by creation will be wrapped up and ended, because the purpose of God has reached its fulfilment, and there will be a new order of things altogether (2 Peter 3:13).

This should bring home to our troubled and uneasy consciences a very real question. Are we sure that we are and shall be part of the completed purpose of God? Or will we be wrapped up in that final cataclysmic disintegration of creation which has such solemn overtones of judgment? Some of the great theological statements regarding creation deserve long meditation. John Calvin affirmed that 'Creation is the theatre of God's glory,' to set forth and to display in a way that is full and understandable, all that is meant by the glory of God, a revealing of His heart as well as His hands. Emil Brunner expressed it, 'As the holy God He wills to glorify Himself in His creation; as the loving God He wills to give Himself to others.' The Westminster Confession of Faith declares, 'It pleased God the Father, Son and Holy Ghost, for the manifestation of the glory of His eternal power, wisdom and goodness, in the beginning, to create, or make of nothing, the world, and all things therein, whether visible or invisible, in the space of six days, and all very good.' (We must not miss the glorious spiritual truth in such statements by diverting our thoughts into a consideration of the exact nature of the six days, whether they are of twenty-four hours as we know them or geological periods. We are not concerned here with how 'days' are measured.)

The picture we have in the Bible is of the whole order of creation coming from and ordered by God. Read Hebrews, 11:3:

> 'By faith we understand that the world was created by the word of God, so that what is seen was made out of things which do not appear.'

It is by faith that we come to understanding, and there is no other way to grasp the truth about creation. It is not by an increase in scientific understanding that we come to faith. The things which can be seen, measured and compiled statistically cannot be explained only in terms of visible factors. No matter how we computerise, analyse and investigate them scientifically, logically or philosophically, they cannot be understood, they cannot be grasped, they cannot be explained apart from this hidden factor which is grasped only by faith. This hidden factor is God, who not only orders creation but orders the whole course of history. This is the God Christians believe in: the God who is presently, here and now, carrying forward the purposes of history to their inevitable and glorious consummation.

The whole order of creation is from God, called into being through the agency of the Eternal Word who is Jesus Christ.

> '...all things were made through Him, and without Him was not anything made that was made' (John 1:3).

A similar affirmation is found in Paul's Letter to the Colossians.

> 'In Him all things were created, in heaven and on earth, visible and invisible, whether thrones, or dominions or principalities or authorities - all things were created through Him and for Him. He is before all things, and in Him all things hold together' (1:16, 17).

By Him all things exist and cohere. Is it too simple an illustration to visualise not merely our little world that we call the Earth, but all the worlds that are, encircled in the great and mighty arms of the living God? That is what the Christian believes. That is what the Word of God declares. Maybe the old negro spiritual has it best, 'He has the whole world in His hand.' Does that frighten us? It does mean that at every corner of daily life we have a God with whom we have to do. It means that wherever we are and whatever we are doing there is a God who is seeking to press His way into our troubled consciences, to challenge us over who we are, and what we are for. The song goes on, 'He has the tiny little baby in His hand.' That is a comfort. But in a sense it is a troubling kind of comfort, because as He knows and holds the little babe, does it not mean also that this great

21

God, Maker of heaven and earth, is a God who knows us through and through and has known us right from the beginning? He is a God who knows the evasiveness of our thinking, who knows that, times without number, He has sought to lay hold upon our life for salvation and we have moved away from Him. But we cannot get away from God. The Psalmist knew that, when he declared that even if he fled to the furthermost corner of the earth, even there God's hand would hold him (Psalm 139:9,10). Of course, in the ultimate analysis, in the real crises of life, it is comfort beyond all words that it is the hand of our God that holds us safe and secure, not the fickle, treacherous hand of circumstances. When we grasp something of the grandeur and glory of the doctrine of God as Creator we begin to see that the centre of the world is never man, and never *can* be man, but is God.

We begin to see God in something of His infinite greatness. We begin to feel God as Someone who is altogether removed from us, remote from us, separate from us, supreme above us, standing over against us. In a sense we must even think of Him as a God out of reach, far removed from the uncertain turmoil of history (and yet, as we have said, never absent and always active), the God who sits above the circle of the earth (Isaiah 40:22); who speaks and it is done (Genesis 1:3); who works and no man can hinder (Isaiah 43:13). This is our God. He is the high and lofty One who inhabits eternity, whose name is holy (Isaiah 57:15). His throne is everlasting and the government is on His shoulder and in His hand (Isaiah 9:6). When we speak in this way there can come upon us a feeling of awe and uncertainty which is similar to fear. But it is not terror, unless we know ourselves to be in defiance of God. The fear of the Lord is the beginning of wisdom (Proverbs 9:10) and it does nothing but good to realise that all things are naked and open to the eyes of Him with whom we have to do (Hebrews 4:13). The God of creation, who is the God of salvation, is also the God of judgment who has appointed the Day of Judgment (Acts 17:31). It is not for nothing that the New Testament says it is a fearful thing to fall into the hands of the living God (Hebrews 10:31).

THE FATHER

We must not fail to recognise that the Almighty God, Maker of heaven and earth, is also the Father. He is not the Father of all men in the sense that all will finally be saved, because all will *not* finally be saved, and all are not members of the family of God. The Bible is quite clear about this. Jesus spoke to a group of people on one occasion, saying as it were, 'You are of your father the Devil. There is neither grace nor faith in you hearts. You have no place for Me. You have no right to call God your Father' (cf. John 8:42-47). How can the God of creation, the God of providence and the God of judgment be a Father? How can God, who is holy and righteous, have for His sons and daughters creatures like us whom He has made, but who have rebelled against Him and refused Him?

God is the Father. Who can fully expound these words? We cannot simply liken God to earthly fathers. Some human fathers are wonderfully lovable in spite of faults but some are neglectful and indifferent while others are cruel, depraved and destructive. How then can we grasp the meaning of God as Father? Jesus said 'He who has seen Me, has seen the Father' (John 14:9 AV). In Hebrews Jesus is spoken of as the exact image of the Father (1:1-3 AV). God, in the person of the only begotten Son, came down into this world that He made, this world in which He had made men and women

23

creatures of choice, creatures of response, creatures of love and not machines. He came down to earth (2 Corinthians 5:19) to the scene of man's sin, failure, rebellion, brokenness, hunger of heart, lostness, stupidity, pride, worldliness and materialistic idolatry. Put it in a different way. 'The Father has sent His Son as the Saviour of the world' (1 John 4:14); 'God (the Father) so loved the world that He gave His only Son' (John 3:16). That is the kind of Father He is. 'When the time had fully come, God sent forth His Son, born of a woman ...... to redeem ...... so that we might receive adoption as sons' (Galatians 4:4,5). God came down in Jesus Christ, and in Jesus He was numbered with the transgressors. He lived the life that man could never live for himself. He fulfilled the law that man could never fulfil. He died the death that man could never dare die. Why was Jesus there doing that? Because He was the gift of the Father to the hungry-hearted, broken, uncertain world of sinners.

Why does God give like that to those who are so unworthy? Because He is the Father. Consider the story Jesus told of the Prodigal Son (Luke 15). Can a true father ever really forget, even if a child rebels; if a child holds the home in contempt; if a child mocks everything that has been treasured in that home and in that family, and contracts out and leaves the home sending never a post-card, never a letter? Can a father ever forget? He will follow the trail of the rebellious child, with his riotings and his pleasuring, to the far corners of the earth. And, if you look back home, the father's hair goes white and the father's face grows lined, because it is the father's heart that grieves and grieves and grieves. God the Father has gone on record saying that He would never forget His children because their names are graven on the palms of His hands (Isaiah 49:14-16).

God is a Father like that: grieving, not simply over the mass of humanity, but grieving over men and women, one by one. God the Father so loved the world that He gave His only begotten Son. The God who is Almighty, the God who is sufficient in Himself, the God who can call worlds into being by the word of His mouth, looks down on a broken besmirched humanity and His heart yearns to gather them, to bring many sons to glory. Because He was a Father of love like that, the Bible says that God spared not even His own Son but gave Him up for us all (Romans 8:32). Little wonder the paraphrase of 1 John 3 says:

> 'Behold the amazing gift of love,
> The Father has bestowed
> On us, the sinful sons of men,
> To call us sons of God!' (Scottish Paraphrases).

God the Father Almighty, Maker of heaven and earth, was prepared to give up that which was the dearest possession of all Heaven, the Son in whom all fullness dwelled, the Son who was ever the delight of the Father's heart. The Father was prepared to give up Him. What for? To get you for Himself (1 Peter 2:9). Has He got you? Has He got, not merely the understanding of your mind, but the faith and the response of your heart and the yielding of your life? We are back with the story of the prodigal's father, who, because of love, had to allow the son to go to live out the fruit of his own choices, and to reap the harvest of sin. But at the same time the father waited, and longed, and I believe he also watched, as God watches for the response of the hearts of men and women. When the father saw the prodigal yet a great way off (what a picture!) he girded his garments around him and he ran. It is a picture of God the Father so eager to have you to be His child that He cannot wait. He ran to meet him, and put his arms around him and called him, 'My son'.

I believe in God, the Father Almighty, Maker of heaven and earth, who for love of me and for my salvation gave up His only begotten Son to the death of the cross, to make it possible that this wandering, broken, uncertain sinner should come to Him and be His child. He made it possible, but He waits for us to say in our hearts, 'This is the God I need. This is the Saviour I need. This is the life for which I hunger. This is certainty; this is salvation. I will arise and go to my Father.'

When we come to the Father through the Son what do we find? He who called the world into being, He who set the stars in their courses, He who rules from eternity to eternity, takes our life into His own hands to hold us in a way that speaks of eternal security. We begin to understand what the Bible means when it says, 'The Lord Jehovah, in whom is everlasting strength, is my Shepherd, I shall not want.'

CHAPTER THREE

JESUS CHRIST, GOD'S SON

The heart of the Christian faith is not a set of doctrinal propositions, however accurate the theology may be. Far less is the heart of the Christian faith found in a set of prescriptions for behaviour, however strict or liberal these prescriptions may be. The heart of the Christian faith is a person, who, in the words of the Apostles' Creed is Jesus Christ, God's only Son, our Lord.

That is the identification and the description of the person who in His life, death and resurrection is the substance of the whole Christian gospel. A Christian is someone who has come in personal faith to Jesus Christ for salvation, and in obedience has yielded to Him for discipleship. To be a Christian is to believe the truth about Jesus Christ the Son of God and then to confess Him, in the sense of committing one's self to Him in a life of faith and obedience.

Becoming a Christian is not a case of satisfying yourself as to the answers to a whole catalogue of intellectual or philosophical questions. There are people whose arguments are brought to an end, whose questions are all answered, who still do not become Christians. It is a case of a vital transaction: a transaction whereby you accept as your own what Jesus Christ the Son of God has done for you, and which you could never do for yourself, namely all that is signified in the word 'salvation'. Let it be stated plainly: strive as earnestly as we may; work and slave for our fellow men, for religious institutions and for the world; be the most kind, most gentle, loving soul that ever walked the face of the earth; *nothing* that we can do can accomplish

27

salvation. It has to be done for us. In this great transaction by which we become Christians, we come to Jesus Christ and accept as a free gift what He has done for us. Since that is the essence of this almighty transaction in which and by which we are saved, it becomes vitally important to know just who this Jesus Christ is and what He has done.

In the Gospel narratives the question is often asked regarding the identity of Jesus, 'Who then is this, that even the wind and sea obey Him?' (Mark 4:41). Who is this? Is not this the carpenter's son? (Matthew 13:55). Who is this who even forgives sins? (Luke 7:49). Sometimes no answer was given. Sometimes a wrong answer was given, as when Jesus was spoken of as Joseph's son. Sometimes a glorious answer was given, as in the words of Peter when he said, 'You are the Christ, the Son of the Living God' (Matthew 16:16). It is fundamental that we should be clear as to who and what this person, Jesus Christ, is.

We are commanded in Scripture to consider Jesus (Hebrews 12:3), and in doing so we find ourselves presented with the person and the power of God's salvation. We are confronted with His rightful authority, His gracious forgiveness, His healing and restoring power and His unqualified call to follow Him. When we fix our thoughts on Jesus we become aware, as Scripture declares, that He and He alone is the way, the truth and the life and that no man comes to God except through Him (John 14:6). We are left in no doubt that there is no other name under heaven given among men whereby we must be saved (Acts 4:12). We are told that God has given Jesus Christ the name above every name to which every knee must bow (Philippians 2: 10). Jesus Christ is the centre and focus of all, and it is of Him that God bears witness saying, 'This is My beloved Son with whom

I am well pleased' (Matthew 3:17; 17:5). This is the Jesus of the Christian gospel, and He is not just a figure of the past (nor a fictional character): He is the same yesterday and today and forever (Hebrews 13:8).

Since all this is so, it becomes necessary to have a formal statement of truth about Jesus Christ, such as we have in the Apostles' Creed. There are four strands of truth here, found in four different names: 1 - Jesus, 2 - Christ, 3 - God's Son, 4 - Our Lord.

JESUS

'Jesus': a name so simple that it can be lisped by the smallest child who comes to church or Sunday School, and yet a name so deep in its depth, and so eternal in its significance that it stretches the most magnificent theological minds in the world. Jesus is essentially a human name, and brings us at once to think of a real man of flesh and blood who actually walked the face of the earth. He is shown as a man we can speak to, knowing that He understands all the fluctuations and variations of human experience. Jesus is no fictitious character, no product of fertile imaginings. This is a real man, a historical character. You cannot deny Jesus. You cannot deny Nero, you cannot deny Hitler, although you have not met either. In one sense you cannot explain why you believe in their existence, but they are testified to by history, and so is Jesus, and the fullest account of that historical person is found in what we call the Gospels: Matthew, Mark, Luke and John.

If you read the Gospels you find a real man, we dare to say an ordinary man, a man tempted and tried, a man who knew what it was to be misunderstood, who knew what it was to stand at the grave of a friend and weep, a man who knew what it was to live in the midst of wicked, perverse, malicious gossip until His heart was almost broken within Him. He was a man with a fellow-feeling for humanity as He beheld them as sheep without a shepherd: a man who could stand on the brow of the hill and look over the city of Jerusalem that had been so diabolically wicked towards Him and weep over the people, because He saw them as men and women who were working out their own destruction. This is what you find when you read the Gospels, a real man, a man of sorrows, acquainted with grief, arrested on false charges, convicted on perjured evidence, mocked, beaten and kicked around more than any protestor or demonstrator within our own generation. We read concerning Jesus in the Old Testament Scriptures (Isaiah 52:14) that in His suffering His very appearance was so marred that He was scarcely recognisable as a man. This is God's man, Jesus, who was led away to the cross.

When you read the story of this 'ordinary' man, you find some astonishing things. People, not just His own supporters but some of His critics, said, 'No man ever spoke like this man!' (John 7:46). He spoke with an authority that they had never known in any other (Matthew 7:29). They had been in places where they had seen with their own eyes that even demons from hell that tormented the lives of men and women obeyed the voice of this man, and came out of their victims (Mark 5:15). What kind of man is this who, in a house, or at the side of a grave, could speak and call the dead back to life? (Mark 5:35, 41, 42; John 11: 43,44). What manner of man is this? He is a real man, a human man. He knew what it was to be tired and thirsty (John 4:6, 7); He knew homelessness (Luke 9:58) and what it was to weep (John 11:35). Never was any man so truly and utterly human as Jesus. But as you read about Him there comes a persuasion that this is more than a mere man. He is Jesus!

CHRIST

This word 'Christ' signifies the same as the word 'Messiah' and the Messiah or the Christ or the Anointed One is the person in whom all the purposes of God centre and find fulfilment. All that God has ever planned, all that God has ever purposed, all that God seeks and desires from eternity to eternity is expressed in, and carried out by this man we call Jesus Christ.

In the mind and heart of God, from the beginning of time to the end of time, as from the beginning of the Bible to the end of the Bible, the centre and fulfilment of everything is Jesus Christ, God's eternal Son, who from the world of eternity came down among men on the platform of history. When Christ came, all the words and works of God were focused coherently, and defined clearly, for men to see. 'The Word was made flesh and dwelt among us and we beheld His glory, the glory as of the only begotten of the Father, full of grace and truth' (John 1:14 A V). God, who had spoken down the ages through prophets and through events of history, spoke finally and conclusively in His Son, who is the key to the understanding of all history and all God's purposes. People say, 'We do not understand about God'. The answer is, look at Jesus! It is recorded that one day one of His own disciples looked at Him and said, 'Show us the Father, (show us God,) and we shall be satisfied'. And Jesus said, 'He who has seen Me has seen the Father' (John 14: 8,9). Does that mean that this Jesus, this real man, this Christ, is God? Yes! (John 4: 25,26;10: 30). God Himself had come down among men as He promised He would. All through the long books of the Old Testament there is the recurring note, the promise of the Messiah, the One who should come. His name Emmanuel means 'God with us'. When you look at Jesus Christ the truth is: God with us! God, whose habitation is eternity, who is infinite and eternal, who is altogether removed from us and altogether other than us, God of might, majesty and power, this God came down among us. And the first sign that this had really happened in history was when a new-born babe cried.

In the Gospel story it is recorded that John the Baptist sent some of his disciples to ask Jesus a question. 'Are you He who is to come, or shall we look for another?' (Matthew 11:3). John, in prison, and his disciples heard about the things that Jesus had been doing and it kindled their spirits within them. Could this be the promise fulfilled? When you are waiting for some important person to come on an official visit there can be a thrill of anticipation. You see various signs of activity. People take up official positions. High-ranking policemen appear. Doors are opened and carpets are rolled out. Everyone is eager. Is he coming? It is a poor illustration but it indicates something of the atmosphere at the time of John the Baptist's question. Taught by the Scriptures they believed God would send His 'Christ', the Messiah, as He had promised. His coming would be the great catalyst to bring to fruition the plan and purpose of God for the salvation of His people. When John and the people heard of the wonderful words and mighty works of Jesus it was understandable that they should ask the question, 'Are you He that should come? Are you the One we have been waiting for? Are you the promised One?' This promised One was the Messiah Himself, in whom, and through whom, all the purposes of God would find their consummation. Little wonder they were excited.

Are you the One that should come, or do we look for

another? These could be the words of any of the people who knew their Old Testament. They knew that Zechariah the prophet, speaking of the hope of the Messiah's coming, said,

> 'Behold thy King cometh unto thee, lowly and riding upon an ass, and upon a colt, the foal of an ass' (9:9 AV).

Now they saw Jesus sitting on the beast riding into Jerusalem and they drew the obvious conclusion. This was their King for whom they had waited. This was the Messiah come to His people. This was the Christ, the anointed One! The Pharisees called on Jesus to forbid such claims for they did not recognise Him as the Christ; but Jesus replied to the effect that if the people were silenced the stones would cry out, because the very stuff of creation was aware of who He was, and why He had come (Luke 19:40).

GOD'S SON

Long years before Jesus was born the prophet Micah spoke:

> 'But thou Bethlehem Ephratah, though thou be little among the thousands of Judah, yet out of thee shall He come forth unto Me that is to be ruler in Israel; whose goings forth have been from old, from everlasting' (Micah 5:2 AV).

Note that the promised One, Jesus, the Christ, the Son of the living God is spoken of as coming from eternity. He is God's Son. On occasions in the Gospel story (Luke 7:48,49; Mark 2:5,7) Jesus spoke publicly and said, 'Your sins are forgiven.' People were shocked. They said, 'No-one can forgive sins except God!' They were right! But they were looking at and listening to God's eternal Son and they did not recognise Him!

The promised One had come. Where had He come from? From eternity. In His great High Priestly prayer, spoken to God the Father just before the final drama of the crucifixion, Jesus said,

> 'Father, glorify Thou Me in Thy own presence with the glory which I had with Thee before the world was made' (John 17:5).

He is Jesus, blessed human name. He is Christ, the promised One, in whom and through whom all the purposes of God find their fulfilment. He is God's only Son. All that God is and all that God has to say to men became flesh and dwelt among us. God, the high and eternal One, infinite and unchangeable, before whose presence even the unfallen angels cover their faces and cry, 'Holy,Holy, Holy, is the Lord God Almighty,' came right down into the context of your life and mine, and we see Him in Jesus Christ, His only Son.

Think of the glorious affirmation of the Christmas carols:

> 'He came down to earth from heaven
> Who is God and Lord of all,
> And His shelter was a stable,
> And His cradle was a stall....' (Alexander)

> 'Who is He, in yonder stall,
> At whose feet, the shepherds fall?
> Tis the Lord, the King of Glory....' (Hanby)

> 'Lo within a manger lies
> He who built the starry skies,
> He who, throned in height sublime
> Sits amid the cherubim...' (Caswall)

What was He doing down here, God's only Son in the stable? God the eternal Son, the One who with the

Father dwelt in the perfect unity of the Holy Spirit in love that was totally sufficient and satisfying from all eternity, what was He doing here? What is the meaning of this 'bereavement' of heaven, this departure of the Son and this visitation of earth? Who is this babe, this man, this teacher, this one who will hang so silently upon the cross? He is God's eternal Son.

> 'And can it be, that I should gain
> An interest in the Saviour's blood?
> Died He for me, who caused His pain -
> For me, who Him to death pursued?
> Amazing love! how can it be
> That Thou, my God, shouldst die for me?'
>
> (Wesley)

That is not what the modern theologians mean when they speak about 'the death of God'. But what an awesome statement it is:

'That Thou, my God, shouldst die for me'.

God's eternal Son came down to earth to die for us and for our salvation.

If you listen to the words of Jesus as they are written in the Gospels you become aware of the fact that He must either be what He claimed to be, or else He was mad, or an impostor, or a blasphemous rogue. He was what He said He was, the Son of God. His words are clear:

'Before Abraham was, I am' (John 8:58).

The Jews were angry and said, 'This man is making himself equal with God' (John 5:18). True, for He was God the eternal Son. He proceeded forth from God, out of the very being of God (John 8:42). God sent Him (Galatians 4:4). That is where He came from. In a real sense we are out of our depth here for we are driven back into the counsels of eternity.

'In the beginning was the Word, and the Word

was with God, and the Word was God. He was in the beginning with God. All things were made through Him, and without Him was not anything made that was made. In Him was life, and the life was the light of men ....And the Word became flesh and dwelt among us ....' (John 1:1-4,14).

The Word was made flesh and dwelt among us. He came to His own and His own received Him not (John 1:11). This is the hideous sin of remaining in unbelief, the sin of not coming to Jesus. It is the spurning of the eternal Son of God, who, though He was rich, for our sakes became poor, that we, through His poverty might be made rich (2 Corinthians 8:9). This One who, being in the form of God, thought it not something to be grasped at to claim His right of equality with God, but humbled Himself, and became obedient unto death, even the death of the cross (Philippians 2:5-8).

OUR LORD

Because He is who He is and has done what He has done for us and for our salvation, Jesus Christ, God's only Son, has every right to claim the Lordship of our lives. After all, He is in every sense Lord of all. The testimony of Scripture is clear. Jesus Christ is Lord of creation, Lord of history, Lord of the church. In everything He stands pre-eminent (Colossians 1:18).

God has made this Jesus, Lord and Christ (Acts 2:36). He has been given the name that is above every name to which every knee shall bow in heaven and earth and under the earth (Philippians 2:9-11). His Lordship is total. He is, in fact, King of Kings and Lord of Lords (Revelation 19:16).

When Paul met this risen, glorious Christ on the road to Damascus (Acts 9: 3-5) he realized at once that he was face to face with One who was rightly Lord. This is fact and it confronts us to challenge us.

You do not negotiate terms with this Jesus. You simply surrender and give Him what is His by right, the Lordship of your life. That should end all compromise and all slowness regarding Christian life and service.

CHAPTER FOUR

BORN OF THE VIRGIN MARY

We have considered the words, 'I believe in God,' discovering that the moment we say 'I believe,' we are not simply giving intellectual assent to the truth but we are committing ourselves on the basis of the truth that we acknowledge. We then considered the kind of God we believe in: God the Father Almighty, Maker of heaven and earth, as He has revealed Himself to us, the record of that revelation being Holy Scripture. We are not left to choose our own kind of God. It is not a matter of preference or fashion. God has made Himself known, leaving us in no doubt whatever as to His nature and character. Then we came to the words 'Jesus Christ, His only Son our Lord,' a title or description in which each word or phrase is significant. This Jesus 'was conceived by the Holy Ghost, born of the Virgin Mary, suffered under Pontius Pilate.'

The Creed is formulated in three distinct paragraphs, the first and the third being comparatively brief. The central paragraph concerns the person and the work of Jesus Christ and it is not by accident that this paragraph is far longer than either of the others, because the message of the Christian gospel begins, centres and ends in the person and work of Jesus Christ. The moment we drift away from that we are into the arid area of uncertainty and confusion. Everything depends on who Jesus is and what He did. All our understanding of doctrine must anchor itself in Him, just as all our interpretation of the Bible, from Genesis at the beginning to Revelation at the end, must be in terms of the person and work of Jesus Christ. This is not an arbitrary statement, but the affirmation that He Himself made to the disciples after the resurrection. In the story of Emmaus (Luke 24:27,44) we read that from Moses, the Prophets and the Psalms He unfolded to His disciples the things concerning Himself. Old Testament and New Testament together form one book with a coherent testimony to the person and work of Jesus Christ. A good and effective way of discerning the nature of the many false and strange sects and religions appearing in our day is to examine what they say about the person of Jesus Christ, the nature and significance of His death on the cross and the historical fact of His bodily resurrection.

Who then is this historical figure called Jesus Christ who claimed to be the Son of God? The Bible shows Him in a three-fold aspect.

The first declaration of identity was made by John the Baptist to his disciples. Pointing to Jesus he said, 'Behold, the Lamb of God, who takes away the sin of the world' (John 1:29,36). Right through the Old Testament from the time of the story of Abraham's willingness to sacrifice his son Isaac (Genesis 22:1-14) the Jews looked to the time when, in the the fullest sense, God would provide the Lamb foreshadowed in Abraham's great affirmation of faith, 'God will provide Himself the Lamb for a burnt offering' (Genesis 22:7,8). The story of the Passover Lamb on the night of the Exodus, the deliverance from Egypt, was yet another confirmation of God's intention (Exodus 12:1-13). God would one day provide *the* Lamb who would be the fulfilment of the symbolic sacrifices of the Old Testament: a Lamb for sacrifice who would take the place and be the substitute for the one who should die. In the fullness of time the man Jesus Christ appeared and the prophet of God pointed to Him saying, 'Behold the Lamb of God'.

The gospel also says of this Jesus, 'Behold the man;'

an expression taken from the story of the arrest and the crucifixion of Jesus (John 19:5 AV). 'Behold the man,' said Pilate, and there Jesus stood, robed and mocked by the men of the world who counted Him as nothing. Behold the man, a true man, man as God planned him to be. He was God's 'proper man' as Luther describes Him.

'Behold your King,' (John 19:14) is the third affirmation, and this was also said by Pilate, who, at first, had serious doubts whether this brutalised, silent man could possibly be royal (John 18:33). But if we read the account of the conversation with Pilate and consider the demeanour of Jesus in and through His mockery of a trial with its public humiliation, we see that He was every inch a King. He was (and is) King of Kings and Lord of Lords whose throne is above every throne. Prophet and Governor spoke truly when they described Jesus as Lamb, Man and King.

We see Jesus, then, in relation to God and in relation to man. We also see Him in relation to time, and in relation to eternity. We see Him again as One who is essentially far removed from and far above all, and at the same time we see Him as One who is down here amongst men, very much one of us. We see Him first in Scripture as the pre-incarnate Christ: He was with the Father in the endless ages of eternity before any worlds were ever made (John 1:1-3). Then we see Him as the incarnate Christ, made flesh amongst men, born of the Virgin Mary. We see Him also as the glorified Christ, for that is what He is now, in the presence of the Father, from whence He first came (Hebrews 9:24).

Who then is this Jesus? To answer that question we are necessarily pushed back in thought into eternity, and that is a concept really beyond us. In spite of all our pride in ourselves we are still hemmed in in terms of yesterday, today and tomorrow, creatures of time and of space. But it was not so with Jesus. Remember the words from His own lips in that great prayer in John, chapter 17, speaking of the glory He had with the Father before the world was created. That is the person who was born in Bethlehem, the incarnate Christ, God's eternal Son, the One who was and is the express image and the exact likeness of the Father. Remember what He said to Philip, (John 14:9) 'He who has seen Me has seen the Father.' This Jesus, God's eternal Son, came down from Heaven. We may not understand fully how this can be, but we must accept the testimony of Scripture. We must not qualify or explain away what the Bible says clearly. The eternal One came down from heaven and was made man for us and for our salvation. In a sense it is very simple. You have it in the Christmas carol, 'Once in Royal David's city':

> 'He came down to earth from heaven
> Who is God and Lord of all,
> And His shelter was a stable,
> And His cradle was a stall' (Alexander).

He was born of Mary, but Scripture makes plain Joseph was not His father (Matthew 1:24,25; Luke 1:34,35). It is simple, and yet at the same time it is such a profound mystery that it has exercised the greatest of intellects for nearly two thousand years.

Who is this Jesus whom we have heard about since childhood, and the preaching of whose name is called the gospel? He is God; nothing other, nothing less; but He is also man. He is true and perfect God; true and perfect man: two distinct natures in indissoluble unity, in one person and personality. We must be very careful here, because He is not a mixture of God and man, giving us a hybrid creature who is neither God nor man. We must

not ever think of Him as being half God and half man.
When reading the Bible we must never fall into the trap
of saying that in one place (the miraculous, perhaps),
Jesus is acting as God but in another place He is acting
as a man. We must not make Jesus a 'split' personality.
He is one coherent person and the Gospel narratives
portray Him as such. He is God. He is man.

Consider the words of the Shorter Catechism:

'The only Redeemer of God's elect is the Lord
Jesus Christ, who, being the eternal Son of God,
became man, and so was, and continueth to be,
God and man in two distinct natures, and one
person, for ever' (S.C. 21).

The Westminster Confession states it more fully:

'The Son of God, the second person in the
Trinity, being very and eternal God, of one
substance, and equal with the Father, did, when
the fullness of time was come, take upon Him
man's nature, with all the essential properties
and common infirmities thereof, yet without sin;
being conceived by the power of the Holy Ghost,
in the womb of the Virgin Mary, of her
substance. So that two whole, perfect and
distinct natures, the Godhead and the manhood,
were inseparably joined together in one person,
without conversion, composition, or confusion.
Which person is very God and very man, yet one
Christ, the only Mediator between God and
man' (Chapter 8:2).

Anything suggesting that Jesus is not truly God must
be rejected totally and utterly, for it is in seeing Jesus
Christ as the mighty Lord of glory that we see Him as our
Saviour and our Lord, and as the mighty Victor who
always causes us to triumph. A weak Jesus would be no
use! Is it not true that even the best of men fail us? Is it

not true that mortal man, even at his highest pinnacle of achievement, even spiritual achievement, fails us? One who is liable to fail is no use as a Saviour for sinners, because we are left with the possibility that an occasion might arise when He is not able to meet our need. But if He is who He claims to be, God the eternal Son, then there is no doubt about His power.

It is also true, however, that people who are filled with power, those who are high and lifted up, tend to become increasingly remote from us. When we are dealing with only limitless power, however glorious, pure and majestic, there is something within us that would make us cringe back and hesitate to approach. We tend to feel, even if we do not say it, that such a great and glorious person is too important to have time to think of insignificant creatures such as we are. Some of the great and successful are in fact forgetful of others and lack both understanding of and sympathy for the ordinary, especially the weak and broken who seem failures. But it is not so with Jesus. He is human: totally human. He is not only mighty to save, He is a man, infinitely tender and understanding.

This is the Saviour whom God has given to us, the great and glorious Victor, who is able to save to the uttermost (Hebrews 7:25 AV) and who, at the same time, is touched with the feeling of our infirmities (Hebrews 4:15 AV). When we behold our Saviour in His Godhead and His manhood, we see both the limitlessness of His power to save and the limitlessness of His compassion and understanding. There are people with heavy hearts, troubled and crushed by a sense of sin, failure and shame, who feel they have no-one to whom they can unburden their hearts. There is one person you can always tell. He will never brush you off as if you did not matter. He will never harden His heart as if He did not care. He will never make you feel a miserable, wretched worm, because whatever the situation, the circumstance, the temptation, the battle, the sorrow or the joy you are experiencing, it says in Holy Scripture that He Himself, the human Son of God, the man Jesus Christ, as a man, tasted that very experience for you, for your sake, and for your salvation. He knows what the power of temptation and the depth of sorrow are. He is truly man.

This then is the Saviour, He who is God and man, sent when God judged that the time was ripe. What humility there is in God, to come down like this! We who are such pompous creatures would not do this, we have too exalted a sense of our own dignity. It was not so when God the Son was born of Mary:

'A stable place sufficed,
The Lord God Almighty, Jesus Christ'

(Rossetti).

The Son of God came down to undergo the experience of being a helpless babe: Almighty, but needing everything done for Him in the total dependence of a newborn baby. He knew all that we mean by the growth of a child. He knew all that we mean by the struggles and the uncertainties of adolescence. This Jesus knew all that we mean (whatever we mean), when we speak of the rigours of manhood. There was not a part of human life that He did not take to Himself. Although He had no sin or failure to be ashamed of Himself, He understood and felt for those who had. He was truly and fully human. He came to do as man for man, all that man had failed to do. All this and more is signified by the phrase, Born of the Virgin Mary.

CONCEIVED BY THE HOLY GHOST

To be born of the Virgin Mary He was conceived by the Holy Ghost. Theologians and philosophers have argued about the mechanics, the significance and the necessity or otherwise of the Virgin Birth for generations, in an attempt to express in terms of logic this glorious mystery. They try, by sheer reason, to hold together all that we mean by the divinity of Christ, the humanity of Christ and the sinlessness of Christ. They say about the phrase, 'Conceived by the Holy Ghost,' that this must be in order that Christ might be preserved from the taint of original sin. But while there was no earthly father there was an earthly mother. And when you deal with this simply in terms of logic, you end up in the position of the Roman Catholic Church with regard to Immaculate Conception. They insist that Mary must somehow or other have come into the world differently, also without sin, so that through her, by the Holy Ghost, the Christ of God could be born a sinless man among men. But there is no suggestion of this complicated explanation or interpretation in the Nativity stories. Indeed Mary speaks of rejoicing in her Saviour, and only sinners need a Saviour. The sinless are in a different category!

Of course it is not the mechanics of this doctrine that matter, but the theology of it, that is, the Word of God concerning it. What then does the Word of God say in this statement concerning His Son, 'Conceived by the Holy Ghost, born of the Virgin Mary'? God says that when the situation was ready for His mighty work of salvation, He Himself took the initiative and acted without the help, the co-operation, the instrumentality of fallen man. God stepped into the sphere of human failure and He Himself took man's place. Man, who had already failed in Adam, was set aside, and God, the mighty Lord Himself, took the initiative, and the appointed Saviour was conceived by God the Holy Ghost. It was a sovereign act of God. It was God who did it because nobody else could. God alone was the One who acted. Man could not be the agent of salvation because he is fallen. It is surely *obvious* that man is fallen. The evidence of the daily newspapers should be sufficient, but fallen man is so proud in his brokenness that even when the whole of experience testifies to his sin and his failure he will not believe it. Fallen man is determined to be self-sufficient. He not only denies the consequences of sin and of the fall, he is determined to work his passage to heaven, to do it himself; but it cannot be done. Broken sinful man in his pride, his incompetence and his inability, was set aide, and God Himself took the initiative and started again. This is the doctrine of the Virgin Birth.

God started again, and began a new humanity headed up in Jesus Christ. That is what it means when we say, 'He was conceived by the Holy Ghost'. No mere creature could ever represent God. If God was to be seen and known in the miserable circumstances of human sin and failure, then God must come Himself - and He did! The Saviour of the human race, the last Adam came. In one sense the Bible really speaks about only two men: the first Adam, who failed, and the last Adam, who came to the fight and to the rescue, conceived by the Holy Ghost, born of the Virgin Mary. Man as the head, man as the strong one, was laid aside, but woman, representing the weaker aspect of humanity, is found taking part. Does it not say in the New Testament that God has chosen the weak things of the world (1 Corinthians 1:27)? Could He have chosen anything weaker than the maiden whose name was Mary, the one who in the simplicity of genuine modesty looked into the face of God and said, 'How can this be, seeing I know not a man?' God answered:

> 'The Holy Ghost shall come upon thee, and the power of the Highest shall overshadow thee: therefore also that holy thing which shall be born of thee shall be called the Son of God' (Luke 1:35 AV).

BORN OF THE VIRGIN MARY

Mary said, 'Be it unto me, according to Thy word'. The whole scheme of salvation was beyond her grasp, outwith her ability, and unique to human experience. It was a plan that would obviously cause hurt to her dear promised husband-to-be and would bring suspicion and shame on them both, and on their families. But faith, simple, uncomplicated and yet strong, responded in willing submission to God and to His plan. 'Behold, the handmaid of the Lord.' It was as if she said, 'Lord, if this is what You want my life's service to be, let it be so.' Perhaps faith saw clearly that if the Saviour was to come, then it must be by a sovereign act of God, by His Holy Spirit, through a human life chosen for that purpose. So, God came down to be one of us in a truly human life.

> 'Veiled in flesh the Godhead see;
> Hail the Incarnate Deity,
> Pleased as Man with man to dwell,
> Jesus our Immanuel' (Wesley).

God's man came down to be one of us, and in human life where man had failed He had, as man, to prevail. The representative and substitute came to do as a man, in the life of man, and for man, all that man had failed to do. There was no compulsion on Him to do it. He did it freely for sinners.

There are two different ways of fulfilling an obligation to a superior. You can try to do it yourself, or you can get another person, someone who is acceptable to your superior, to do it for you. Think of the superior as being God, the God of the Law, with its commandments, prohibitions, requirements, challenges, and thundering warnings of judgment upon all who fail. In the issue of salvation and the broken law you cannot do it yourself. Can you do and be all that God requires without one single flaw or defect from beginning to end? 'No human being will be justified in His sight by works of the law' (Romans 3:20). Can you find anyone else to do it for you? But all others are in the same boat as yourself. Does that mean that if we cannot do it ourselves, and no other man can do it for us, there is no hope? Is there no-one who can meet the requirements and demands of God for us? Is there no-one who, as a man, can do this that is required of man? An angel is no use; he cannot be a man. Is there no-one? There is only Jesus, and God sent His Son to be the Saviour of the world.

God Himself came right down into human life to do Himself what was needed. Being found in fashion as a man, He humbled Himself, and as a man He went the whole way into human life and its consequences. People sometimes say, 'You don't really know how far down I've gone.' Maybe not. But I know this, that God, in the man Christ Jesus, went down into the deepest depths of human brokenness so that not a mortal man or woman on the face of the earth can say, 'Because of my sins and my experience I am beyond the reach of God'. In Jesus Christ, God was touched with the feeling of our infirmity. That word 'touched' is a wonderful one. Have you ever tried to speak to someone who has been deeply hurt or grievously bereaved? As you have seen the sorrow in their faces and have tried to speak to them, your whole heart has ached within you, and there seems to be something in your throat, almost choking the words back. You are touched with the feeling of their infirmity. Now God came down, a man among men, to be touched with the feeling of your infirmity.

In the Epistle to the Hebrews 4:15 we read of Jesus who 'in every respect has been tempted as we are, yet without sinning'. In Hebrews 2:18 we read that, 'He Himself has suffered and been tempted.' Yes, He was a perfect, sinless man. That is why He knew to such infinite degree the pain and the agony of temptation. Only those who resist learn the terrible power of sin. When a mighty wind is blowing it is one thing to turn your back on it, but another thing to turn round and to walk into the very teeth of the gale. That is what Jesus did in terms of human experience, and human temptation. He met the full force of temptation but never yielded. He did it as a man. He knows what it is to go through it. He did not need to do this for Himself. He did it for us.

SUFFERED UNDER PONTIUS PILATE

He suffered under Pontius Pilate. This dates the event and emphasises that the death of Christ was a once-for-all historical happening. In one sense, in that phrase about the Roman governor at the time of the crucifixion, you see a figure of God the eternal Judge. What were the two things that Pilate did? He said and did what God did. First of all, Pilate pronounced this victim to be sinless, saying, 'I find no fault in this man.' Then, having pronounced Him sinless, he delivered Him to death. That is exactly what God did when He looked down upon the man Jesus Christ, calling Him, 'My beloved Son, in whom I am well pleased'. God pronounced Him sinless and then delivered Him up to death. God spared not even His own Son, the Son that He had sent in the likeness of sinful flesh, and as a sacrifice for sin. God took this One and 'made Him to be sin' (not a sinner) for us (2 Corinthians 5:21). God caused the sin and iniquity of us all to meet upon Him. God took the sins of mankind and piled them up on Jesus the sinless One, until, looking down from the glory of heaven to the cross of Calvary, God saw not His only Son, but the sins of the world, and the judgment of God fell upon them, in Him. God delivered this man whose name is Jesus to the death of the cross, to the judgment of sin, and to the penalty of sin, for you and for me.

That is the truth of the gospel, expressed in brief compass and in simple terms. It is all summed up in the person of Jesus Christ, conceived by the Holy Ghost and born of the Virgin Mary, for the specific purpose of suffering and dying on the cross by the human decision of Pilate the Roman Governor. The truth is, of course, that Jesus was sent by God and delivered up according to the definite plan of God (Acts 2:23). It was God who laid on Him the iniquity of us all (Isaiah 53:6). Pilate had no power to send Jesus to His death (John 19:11), neither had the religious authorities. They all acted under the sovereign, saving providence of God (Acts 4:26-28), but the actions of men were wicked (Acts 2:23). History has not been allowed to forget that Jesus was crucified under Pontius Pilate.

CHAPTER FIVE

CHRIST CRUCIFIED

The story of the crucifixion and death of Jesus Christ is found recorded in detail in the four Gospels, Matthew, Mark, Luke and John. The meaning and significance of the event is declared and expounded throughout the whole of the New Testament. When we consider Jesus Christ and Him crucified we must affirm at once it is not the *story* of the crucifixion that is the Christian gospel but the *message* of that crucifixion. It is not the mere narrative of the historical happening but the significance and the explanation of that narrative that constitutes the gospel.

It is important to grasp this at the outset because there is confusion even among religious people over the meaning of the cross. An intelligent, successful businessman, a churchgoer, made this astonishing statement: 'What I like about the story of the cross is that there is no theology in it'. Nothing could be further from the truth. The man was drawn to and moved by the story of the crucifixion but his reaction was emotional. The story has a great appeal to all kinds of people, which is why you find some under the influence of drink singing 'The Old Rugged Cross'. The story has an appeal and a fascination. It grips people and makes them feel better, which may be why some use crosses as necklaces. The story of the cross has the kind of fascination that affects the thinking and the feeling of the most astonishing types of people, and you find gravestones in the form of a cross standing over the graves of some reprobate unbelievers.

The Bible is quite clear that the message of the cross is not primarily intended to stir emotions of pity or admiration. The message of the cross of Jesus Christ is not merely that the cross is a demonstration of the extent of God's love, although it is that:

> 'God shows His love for us in that while we were yet sinners Christ died for us' (Romans 5:8).

We do not proclaim a message telling of the extent of God's love in order to appeal to people to be a little better, a little kinder, a little more honourable. Many people do not see why they should be kinder or more honourable; they do not want to be! Nor is the message of the cross of Jesus Christ simply the story of the most magnificent example of self-sacrifice that the world has ever known, by which example we are called upon to do our little bit for humanity, to send a pound to the starving through Christian Aid before we spend fifty pounds on our own food and drink in celebration of Christmas. Inside and outside the church we have been guilty of sentimentalising the story of the cross to such an extent that the theology of the cross has been forgotten.

The Bible states quite clearly that the cross is a place where something unique was done, something that had never been done before, something that never needs to be done again, something done once, for all and for ever. It was done by the initiative of God, through His only Son our Lord and Saviour Jesus Christ. At the cross there was something accomplished, a mighty work carried out not by men, who were only the guilty instruments of the actual crucifixion, but by God. It was a unique event. Never has there been, never can there be anything like it in the whole span of human history, nor in the endless ages of eternity. It was a work totally and utterly complete in itself. It was final and conclusive. That is why, before He died, our Lord and Saviour Jesus Christ cried out, not in a whimper of exhaustion or in complaint, but in notes of absolute triumph, 'It is finished!' When the work He had come to do had been done, when the great event had been consummated, when nothing else was left to be done, Jesus called out in a loud voice so that all in heaven and earth and hell could hear, 'Finished!' Then He dismissed His spirit and He died.

What was finished? What was this unique non-repeatable work that was done on the cross by God through Jesus Christ? The Bible says:

> 'God was in Christ, reconciling the world unto Himself' (2 Corinthians 5:19 A V).

We have the same kind of statement in 1 Peter 3:18:

> 'Christ also died (suffered) for sins once for all, the righteous for the unrighteous, that He might bring us to God.'

Can we not come to God apart from this? No! Right from the opening chapters of the Book of Genesis, when man was cast out from Paradise, the angel of judgment was set at the gates of the Garden with a flaming sword turning in every direction to bar the way so that sinful man could not return into the presence of God. But Jesus Christ suffered for sins, the just for the unjust, to bring us to God. This is the heart, the focal point of the whole Bible. This is the good news that constitutes the Christian gospel: something has been done for us, by God in Jesus Christ, something that we could never do for ourselves.

What has been done for us? It is the complete work of salvation. It is this objective work, the divine transaction of the cross, that distinguishes the Christian message from mere religion. Religion is essentially something that *you* do but the Christian gospel is about something that has been done *for you*. Many people are attracted to religion because, among other things, it appeals to their vanity. It gives them something to do. They can work, serve on a committee, parcel up clothes for refugees, have a bread and cheese lunch and give money to a good cause. They can support the church. That is religion, and people like it because it is something that *they* can do. But say to religious people that their religion cannot bring them to God, that their service for men and their work for institutional religion cannot save their souls, tell them they need to lay all that down and come empty-handed, like a beggar, to the One who has done it *all* for them, and accept salvation gift-wise from God and you will find that the pride in their hearts says, 'No!' This is why many religious people, including some who go to church Sunday by Sunday, are still not Christians. Their hearts and hands are too full of religion , too full of what *they* do. Such religious people may love to sing Toplady's great hymn, Rock of Ages:

'Not the labours of my hands
Can fulfil Thy law's demands;
Could my zeal no respite know,
Could my tears for ever flow,
All for sin could not atone;
Thou must save, and Thou alone.'

But they do not believe that this is in fact the only way of salvation.

The Christian gospel is all about something that has been done, and which can become ours only by being accepted as a gift. A cultured lady, after an evangelistic meeting, spoke to the evangelist and said, 'Sir, I have tried so hard.' By the inspiration of the Spirit of God the evangelist simply said, 'It is not trying, it is trusting.' The dear woman had never seen that until then. But she did see it, and believed and became a Christian.

When we speak like this we begin to see that the Christian gospel is indeed gloriously simple. Yet at the same time it is too deep for us to plumb,

'Amazing love! how can it be
That Thou, my God, shouldst die for me?'

But He had to *die* for us, for there was no other way by which He could bring us to Himself. When we speak about the cross like this I think we see the blasphemy of the utterance of the man who said, 'God will forgive, that is His job.'

What is it in the human situation in relation to God that makes the cross necessary? What was dealt with at the cross? The Bible is very clear about this. From the beginning of the Book of Genesis to the end of the Book of Revelation there is reasoned out, demonstrated and brought home to us personally, the *fact* of human sin.

'There is none righteous, no, not one.'

'That every mouth may be stopped, and all the world may become guilty before God.'

'All have sinned, and come short of the glory of God' (Romans 3: 10,19,23 AV).

There was an old Christian woman once dealing with a young man who was too conceited to accept this doctrine concerning himself, but she knew how to deal with it. She got out her Bible, turned up Romans Chapter 3, and asked the man to read it slowly. He began to read, 'It is written, there is none righteous, no, not one,' and the woman put her hand on to his arm and said, 'Except you.' She did this with him right through the passage adding her comment, 'Except you,' again and again until, in the end, the man saw, and accepted that there were in fact no exceptions.

'There is none righteous, no, not one.' That is the predicament. The human plight lies in the fact that we are sinners: sinners in the sight of God, guilty, vile and helpless, with absolutely nothing to commend us to God. When I was at university one of my student colleagues came to church for a few Sundays and then refused to come back. I was determined to find out why. I pressed him for an answer, and his face was red with anger as he spat out the words, saying, 'I am not going back there to listen to that man calling me a sinner.' He meant it. He never did go back.

Be clear about this: the first step in becoming a Christian is simply to step into the place of the sinner, the sinner who *is* nothing, and *has* nothing except his sin, and who can *do* absolutely nothing to help himself. People protest that they are not as bad as that. None of us are, in practice, as bad as we could be because of various restraints. But the standard is not the lives of other people. We do not compare ourselves with them; the standard is life as Jesus lived it. The truth is that we are sinners by nature, choice and practice (Ephesians 2:1-3). This is what the Bible says, and it is in relation to sin that Jesus Christ came. This is the affirmation of the Christmas Story: 'You shall call His name Jesus, for He will save His people from their sins' (Matthew 1:21). This is what He came for. We have the message right through the Bible. In Hebrews 9:26: 'He (Christ) has appeared once for all at the end of the age (in the fullness of history) to put away sin by the sacrifice of Himself.'

The abiding problem is sin and the record of sin that stands against us. There is in the Bible (Colossians 2:14 AV) a verse that speaks about 'the handwriting that was against us'. When I worked as a bank clerk one verse of the Bible used to bring a real quiver to my soul. It is in the Book of Revelation: 'And the books were opened.' When the Bank Inspectors came, if there was a single figure or fact out of place in the books they would find it, and they would find out who was responsible! There are also the books of God. The story is there: the handwriting that is against us. Would that we believed it! Think of the words from the poem 'Omar Khayyam':

'The Moving Finger writes; and having writ
Moves on: nor all thy piety nor Wit
Shall lure it back to cancel half a line,
Nor all thy Tears wash out a Word of it'
(Fitzgerald).

The Bible puts it more briefly, 'God requireth that which is past' (Ecclesiastes 3:15 A V). That is the plight of man the sinner, guilty before God, estranged from God, at enmity with God, in bondage to what we call sin. We are sinners by nature who have sinned in thought, word and deed. When conscience troubles us and we try to reform, we begin to discover that we have neither freedom nor power. We are held captive. We are in the power of sin and it has dominion over us. We need deliverance as well as forgiveness, someone to deal with the guilt of sin and to break the power of sin. This is what was accomplished by the death of the Saviour.

Even if human sin could be removed, the problem would still not be solved. All through the Bible we find that over against the fact of sin there is another fact. 'The wrath of God is revealed against all ungodliness and wickedness of men' (Romans 1:18). There is here a double predicament: the sin of man and the wrath of God; both stand revealed. We are not speaking of the wrath of God in terms of our wrath, which is so often just a blaze of anger, unprincipled, unbalanced and unreasonable. The wrath of God is a settled disposition of anger on the part of a God who can never be reconciled to evil. Sin creates a situation of wrong in relation to God, to ourselves and to others. Sin is not static, not the kind of thing concerning which you can say, 'That's it done.' That is it only *begun*. There is a sense in which you could think of a pure white canvas representing the righteous heart, purpose and desire of God, and human sin comes along and splashes the canvas. The mark is there and it remains. Faced with the fact and the effect of human sin, the disposition of the righteous God is one of anger and His wrath is revealed. If you think this through you will see that if there is any doubt about the wrath of God, the implacable disposition of God towards all unrighteousness, then the whole constitution of righteousness in this world crumbles to dust. If God is not against evil, who is?

There can be no forgiveness simply by ignoring sin. There must be a removing of sin, a taking away of sin; there must be a sin-bearer upon whom the whole hideous thing can be loaded that he might take it away. At the same time there must also be a turning aside of the righteous wrath of the living God. This double work is exactly what was done at the cross. The death of Jesus Christ on the cross was not merely something *allowed* by God: it was something *done* by God. There is a story of a little lad who looked at a painting of the crucifixion for a long time and eventually said, 'Why did God allow it?' The reply was, 'God did it, my son'. God was in Christ, reconciling the world to Himself. Was God prepared to bruise and to crush His only Son, the Son of His Love, the focus of all we mean when we say 'God is love'? Yes. Read it in Isaiah, chapter 53. It pleased the Lord to bruise Him. He was wounded for our transgressions. He was bruised, crushed, for our sins, and with His stripes we are healed.

The Bible says, 'God made Him to be sin for us'. It was not for Himself that He died because He did not need to die. Indeed such was this man Jesus, such was His life free from all sin, that He could have moved forward *as a man* and taken His place in Heaven by right. There was nothing in Jesus to exclude Him from Heaven. His sufferings were not for Himself: God made

Him to be for sin for us (2 Corinthians 5:21). The picture seems to be of God taking sin as a filthy stinking robe, with a stench that is revolting, and wrapping it round the spotless Son. Have you ever seen sin in some of its hideous, hellish manifestations? Have you seen the ravages of sin in a human life and, when you have seen it, have you felt something cringing within you? Almost, in spite of yourself, you seem to draw back from it. If you who are a sinner yourself feel like that about sin, what do you think was the reaction of the Son of God, who had the filthy thing itself wrapped round about Him? Think of what it cost Him to be the sin-bearer.

God made Him a curse for us. The Bible says, 'Cursed is everyone who hangs on a tree.' In the name of the broken law, God pronounced the curse of judgment on Jesus and left Him alone bearing human sin, your sin, my sin, not only the gruesome sins of the flesh, but the pride of the heart, the pride of life, the cold cruel calculating spirit that can hurt people with sadistic delight. The old negro spiritual asks, 'Were you there when they crucified my Lord?' The answer is 'Yes.' But there is a deeper question. Was God there? Yes, God was in Christ, reconciling the world to Himself, and that is why Jesus died. A young man said, 'I was brought up in church and Bible class; I heard lots of sermons about God, but it was only a very short time ago that I discovered Jesus died for me.' What a condemnation of the Christian church! Did you know that Jesus Christ died for you?

To focus our thoughts on the significance of the death of Jesus Christ think of some of the words used in Scripture. Romans 3:24 speaks of 'redemption', a word that comes from the ancient Roman slave market. The picture is of a helpless slave standing there manacled, with no freedom, no life, no identity, nothing: sold into slavery. What a picture of sin! But a Roman citizen, a free man who has the necessary resources and rights comes into the market and stops before him. The freeman, in spiritual terms Jesus of course, stops, looks at the slave, pays the price, buys the slave out of slavery, and leads him away to newness of life and freedom. He cleanses the slave, He re-clothes the slave, He restores to the slave his dignity as a person and He also gives the slave freedom. The slave might well ask, 'Am I really free?' Yes, he is and that is what Jesus did upon the cross. He paid the price of your redemption to set you free from sin, from death and from hell. When Someone does that for you, you look into His face and say, 'Master, I am Your slave for the rest of my days'.

Another word used is 'propitiation', a difficult word (1 John 2:2, 4:10 AV). It comes from the Old Testament sacrifices, and seems to be linked with the story of the Tabernacle, where the Israelites worshipped. At the very heart of the Tabernacle there was the Ark of God, a box in which were the two tables of the law of God, given by God, through Moses; a broken law that condemned the people. It was a judgment seat. But on the Day of Atonement each year, the High Priest, representing all the people, and bearing in a vessel the blood of the sacrifice that had been shed for sin, entered into that curtained-off area, the inner shrine, the presence of God. There on the judgment seat he sprinkled the blood of atonement for sin so that men could draw near to God and be accepted. That is but the symbol. We are speaking, not of the blood of beasts but of Jesus, who, the Bible tells us, made peace through the blood of His cross. The judgment has been met.

The next word is 'reconciliation'. We sing about it in exultant tones at Christmas, 'God and sinners reconciled,' brought together again, because all the hindrances, all the barriers have been removed by God. In the story of the Garden of Eden, after man had sinned, God came searching longingly for man, saying, 'Where are you?' Man was lost. When man heard the voice of God he hid, because his sins were between him and God. He knew he was estranged from God; he knew he was in the wrong; he knew God had the right to be angry. People sometimes say, 'I have nothing against God,' but that is not the point. Has God got anything against *us*? The thing that God has against us, that which grieves Him and angers Him more than anything else is this: God has sent His only Son Jesus Christ into the world to die on the cross to take away our sins, that we might be reconciled to Him, but we neither open our hearts nor yield our lives to the Saviour who died like that for us.

God was in Christ, reconciling the world to Himself, not imputing, not reckoning, our trespasses to our account. Think of the illustration we used from the inspection of books. Remember Colossians 2, which speaks of Jesus Christ taking the hand-writing that is against us, taking it out of the way and nailing it to the cross. I like to think of the mighty Saviour going to the one who keeps the Book of God and saying, 'Give Me the page that bears the name of George Philip, with all the record of his transgressions, his failures, his wrongs against men, against himself, against Me, and against God.' He takes the page out of the book and nails that condemning document to the tree, as He is nailed there Himself. The trespasses and all the record of them being taken away and the price having been paid, this particular sinner can come back to God.

The last word is 'justification'. Justified means, 'Declared to be righteous.' It is God who justifies. It is an act of His free grace in Jesus Christ. No charges remain on the sheet. The condemned cell that held you as a convicted sinner is now open and you are free to go, because Jesus Christ died to pay the full price of your sin.

> 'Justification is an act of God's free grace, wherein He pardons all our sins, and accepts us as righteous in His sight, only for the righteousness of Christ imputed to us, and received by faith alone' (Shorter Catechism 33).

What have we to do? There is absolutely nothing for us to do. It has all been done. We must accept it by faith. An old Sunday School teacher was trying to bring home the lesson of the free gift of God's salvation in Jesus Christ to a class of boys. Perhaps he felt he had not got through to them, but suddenly he had an inspiration. Unbuckling his gold watch, and holding it out to the first boy, he said, 'Here you are, son, here is a gift for you.' The boy laughed, being embarrassed. The teacher offered it to the next one, and the next one. One little fellow was watching all this and when it came to his turn he put out his hand and took the watch. As the teacher rose to go, the rest of the lads said, 'But, sir, he is not getting to keep it?' 'Yes,' said the teacher, 'it was offered to all of you. You all had the offer of it, but he was the only one who took it'. Now it is not a watch that is offered to us: it is a crucified Saviour. He is offered; is He accepted? The work of salvation, remember, is complete.

> 'Bearing shame and scoffing rude,
> In my place condemned He stood,
> Sealed my pardon with His blood:
> Hallelujah! What a Saviour' (Philip Bliss).

CHAPTER SIX

CHRIST RISEN

Our consideration of the resurrection of our Lord Jesus Christ begins with the words of the Creed, 'Jesus Christ... was crucified, dead and buried; He descended into hell; the third day He rose again from the dead.'

In 1 Corinthians 15, that classic statement of the resurrection, it is affirmed very clearly that if Jesus Christ has not been raised from the dead, if there is in fact no resurrection, then there is nothing at all. There is no gospel, no Christian message, and the whole of Christianity is a fraud and a delusion. We are left with absolutely nothing to human experience save to eat, drink and be merry for tomorrow we die. If there is no physical resurrection of Jesus Christ, and in Him no resurrection of the dead, then all that men can do is to live their lives, making them as merry as is humanly possible so that hopefully they will have no time even to think about death or dying.

If there is no resurrection from the dead, then the thoughts of dying and death are the most desolating and demoralising factors in the whole of human experience. What point is there in anything, if in the end we get put in a box, dumped into the ground, covered with earth and left to rot? Is that all there is to life? If Christ is not risen there is nothing at all. At every funeral service there should be a gracious but clear affirmation of this eternal truth. What does Scripture say?

'If a man die shall he live again?' (Job 14:14).

'It is appointed unto men once to die, but after this the judgment' (Hebrews 9:27).

'There shall be a resurrection, both of the just and unjust' (Acts 24:15 A.V.).

'Give diligence to make your calling and election sure' (2 Peter 1:10 A.V.).
For there is one name, even the name of Jesus,

'And there is salvation in no one else, for there is no other name under heaven, given among men by which we must be saved' (Acts 4:12).

'Jesus said, "I am the resurrection and the life; he who believes in Me, though he die, yet shall he live, and whoever lives and believes in Me shall never die" ' (John 11:25,26).

These are the undergirding fundamental facts that should hold us steady in the midst of all this temporary life that rushes on so predictably to what we call death.

But the clever people of the world would say, 'How can we be sure of all these things? How can we be sure of the reality of the world to come? How can we be sure of the power and sufficiency of Jesus Christ to hold us in and through death and to bring us to God?' What uncertainty many people live with! What is it then that transforms, or should transform, the lives of people who call themselves Christians? What is it that transforms life as it did for the disciples after the death of Jesus on the cross? What is it that gives dynamic, drive and purpose to life? What is it that sends us out into the world with a message to proclaim? What is it that thrills the soul and fills the heart? It is this: Christ is risen! This statement, so simple yet so profound, is what electrified the disciples after the cross, and sent them out into the world willing to be torn asunder, massacred and brutalised, caring nothing for the cost if only they might proclaim the name of Jesus, because He was alive from the dead. All that is meant by death had lost its power.

CHRIST REALLY DIED

Consider the Gospel records and you will see how, time after time, the point is made emphatically that Jesus really died. He was not taken down from the cross *as if* He had died. He was not in a swoon. He was not unconscious. He was *dead*.

Look at the account of the first Easter Day in Luke 24:1-12. The women went to the grave expecting to find nothing but proof of death. As they walked they worried about how they would be able to move the large stone at the mouth of the grave (Mark 16:3). They went prepared with spices and ointments to anoint the dead body of the Lord, and when they reached the tomb and discovered it was empty they were perplexed by the absence of the body, the corpse they had expected to find. It was not there! While they dithered (it is amazing how we usually prefer to dither rather than to believe), two heavenly messengers came and asked, 'Why seek ye the living among the dead? He is not here. He has risen' (Luke 24:5; Matthew 28:6). The Jesus Christ they knew, who had lived and died, had now risen from the dead as in fact He had said He would (Matthew 16:21). The angels said, 'Now go and tell'. The women went and told, but the disciples also were unwilling to believe.

Remember these were men and women who had lived with conflict, with death and with defeat. When Jesus was buried they went into secret hiding-places, shuttered the windows and bolted the doors, because they were terrified thinking about what would happen next at the hands of wicked men.

Think of the position on that Friday night of the

unbelieving men: the leaders of the Jews, the Scribes, the Pharisees, the Roman Authorities, all those whose one concern had been to get rid of Jesus. The civil and ecclesiastical powers, representative of the organisation of anti-Christ in this world, inspired by the Devil himself, had done their worst and had apparently succeeded. They thought they had achieved the end of the person, words and work of Jesus, and, on the face of it, all the evidence was on their side. The man who had hung on the cross had been certified as dead by the Roman Authority; the fact of death was confirmed by a spear being plunged into His side (John 19:34); the death certificate had been written out and signed; and the body had been laid in a grave. Was that not evidence enough that they had got rid of this pestilential, interfering Jesus Christ who would not leave their lives alone? To all appearances, the Jesus movement had collapsed. The disciples had all run away and left Him on the cross, alone apart from one or two and a few of the womenfolk.

Jesus was certified as dead and was buried. Just in case of any unforeseen accidents (notice that evil is never sure of itself, never at peace), the Jewish leaders had the tomb sealed and guarded to make sure the disciples would not try to steal the body and so 'arrange' a resurrection (Matthew 27:62-65). All unwittingly they were making sure that the world throughout its future history would know that the resurrection was a fact and not a fiction. The tomb was sealed by the enemies of Christ, and guarded at their request. Nobody could possibly get near it. But on the third morning the body was not there.

Over against the unbelievers, think of the believing men, the disciples, and you will see that they thought much the same as the wicked men. They thought that Jesus was dead, His voice silenced, His work cast down,

66

and everything finished. They had no thought at all of removing the body in order to prove their case. But the disciples mourned while the others gloated. In spite of having been told in advance that the Son of Man must suffer and die, and the third day rise from the dead, they had failed to grasp the truth, they had failed to stand upon it, they had succumbed to appearances. Their hopes were ended, they had run away, their thoughts were in turmoil, and all they were concerned with was to wait until the end of the Sabbath day, when they would make their way to the graveyard to pay their respects to their dead leader. Then they would go back to the desolation and uncertainty of life, to struggle with circumstances, to struggle with temptations, and in the end to crumple and die. Their hopes had been dashed to such an extent that when the news began to filter through that Jesus was alive from the dead they could not believe it. It seemed to them like idle tales (Luke 24:11). But they could hardly have been more wrong. Jesus was not dead.

HE DESCENDED INTO HELL

Crucified, dead, buried, He descended into hell. No one really knows what that statement means. We can only speculate about it, and speculative theology can be a dangerous thing. But this much is certain: in the period between His death and His resurrection, when wicked unbelievers gloated in their triumph, and when devoted disciples mourned in their disappointment, evil had no cause to rejoice. Christ descended into Hades, into the place of the dead, the place of the departed, the mysterious, unknown, unmeasurable world. What happened? I think that when Jesus died and descended into hell, the whole realm of death, the grave and darkness simply flamed with light, and all the powers of death and darkness were absolutely baffled. They were faced with a situation they could not deal with. On every other occasion, the realm of death and the grave, call it what you will, that whole kingdom of darkness waits with eager triumph for the last fitful breath to flicker out of our human body, and then death snatches its prey, as it has a right to snatch every man and woman whose life is marked with sin, for the wages of sin is death (Romans 6:23). But when Jesus went down into the realm of darkness, death and the grave, that realm discovered that in its kingdom there was now a man who had no sins of His own, and these powers had no means of holding Him. It was not possible that death could hold this man (Acts 2:24). Make it vivid. Think of Jesus standing there in the face of the powers of darkness and challenging them, 'Hold Me if you can! What claim have you on Me?'

They had none. He died bearing a burden of sin, but it was not His own sin. We need to think of Jesus in His death descending into hell, carrying majestically the great load of human sin whose price had been paid, and casting it down into the jaws of death, saying, 'This is your booty. There is your prize. Take it.' Then He turned His back on the realm of darkness and the grave and strode majestically back into the world of men.

This is why we sing in the metrical version of the 23rd Psalm:

> 'Yea, though I walk in death's dark vale
> yet will I fear none ill:
> For Thou art with me; and Thy rod
> and staff me comfort still.'

When a believer goes right down into death, he marches so close behind the mighty victor Christ that he is right down and through to the other side, and death is left gaping in astonishment. Isn't that a gospel to preach to people who are afraid of dying? We sing at Easter, as our hearts should sing every day if we believe the gospel of the resurrection:

'O death, we defy thee!
A stronger than thou
Hath entered thy palace;
We fear thee not now!' (W. C. Plunket).

O death, we would not challenge you by ourselves, but in Christ we defy you!

When Jesus Christ was crucified, dead and buried, and He descended into hell, the whole spirit world shook to its foundations. Let us be quite clear. There *is* a world of angels, spirits and the Devil. We must not lapse into sheer materialism. This visible world is not all there is, but there is beyond and beside it a great unseen, largely unknown world, vaster and fuller than anyone has yet begun to comprehend. For that reason, I for one would never make mockery of those who speak of apparitions and such things as spiritualistic seances. There are frauds, no doubt, but the world of 'spirits' is dangerous and real. We must not trifle with it. But when Jesus was crucified, dead and buried, He descended into hell, and the whole world of spirits shook as He entered and passed through in the triumphal procession of a conqueror. 'He preached to the spirits in prison' (1 Peter 3:19). He heralded, He proclaimed or announced (He did not evangelise), He declared the message of His victory to the spirits in prison.

What was that message? We can only speculate! He descended into hell to proclaim to those reserved unto doom the certainty of judgment. That is what John Calvin says, and of course the death and the resurrection of Jesus Christ did set the seal of inevitable judgment upon evil and unbelief. Others say that Jesus proclaimed to the spirits of the saints of earlier ages that the day they had waited for had come. Remember how Moses and Elijah appeared to Jesus on the Mount of Transfiguration, speaking about the death that He should accomplish (Luke 9:31). All of the Old Testament saints were waiting for that triumphant death and resurrection of Jesus Christ to seal their everlasting blessedness. Others again say He descended into that unknown world to proclaim His victory.

When He descended into the world of departed spirits He must have met there the man we call the dying thief. Jesus had said to him, 'Today, thou shalt be with Me in Paradise'. Can you imagine Jesus Christ looking with a smile into the face of that man who had repented at the last moment and saying, 'I told you! The victory is Mine, and because it is Mine, it is yours. Blessed indeed are you this day.'

This much is sure, in the unseen but real world of spiritual beings and spiritual issues Christ heralded His triumph. He was the King; He was the Victor. And on the third day, having declared His triumph in the world of spirits, He broke into the world of men and declared the same message.

CHRIST ROSE AGAIN FROM THE DEAD

If we really believed the resurrection message, we would begin to turn the world upside down. Perhaps the fact that we are not turning the world upside down signifies that we have hardly begun to believe that Jesus Christ is really alive from the dead. What did the heavenly messenger say to the women on the first Easter Day? 'Why do you seek the living among the dead?' (Luke 24:5).To look at some people's faces and bearing in the church on a Sunday, you would get the impression that they still believe that Jesus is dead. Look at the cross. It is empty! That is why we must have nothing to do with crucifixes that portray Christ still hanging on the cross. He is *not* still on the cross! The cross is empty. Look at the sepulchre; it is empty! Where is He, this man that was nailed to the cross? He is risen from the dead, as He said it would happen. He faced and met human sin and divine judgment and paid the penalty to the uttermost, and now He has risen in triumph over sin, death and every power in earth and hell. There is no power greater than this mighty One whose name is Jesus, who is alive for evermore, and who is able to save to the uttermost of time, to the uttermost of eternity, to the uttermost of experience and need, all those who come to God by Him. There is nothing that the risen Jesus Christ cannot do for us.

To the frightened and depressed disciples the news brought by the women seemed too good to be true at first, as the two on the Emmaus road explained to the unrecognised risen Christ (Luke 24:19-24). Only gradually did it begin to penetrate the disciples' dull minds and irresponsive hearts that Jesus Christ, who had died on the cross, who had been buried in the grave, was in fact alive and in the midst of them. Once that fact was realised there emerged a stream of vibrant enthusiasm and conviction that so notably marked the life of the early Christian church.

Christ was risen! He was alive! To begin with, the resurrection was not a theological statement, although that came as the disciples began to think through more and more the implications of the fact of the resurrection. It was first of all, to these disciples, a thrill of victory. They had not expected it! They had thought all was lost. But it had happened, as He said it would happen. Then, as they began to be aware that all the other things He said were also true, their hearts simply thrilled within them, and they went through the world like wildfire telling everybody, 'Jesus Christ the Son of God came into the world. He died for our sins. He has risen from the dead, triumphant.' As they proclaimed this truth, every shred of the gloom of failure and defeat was banished from their lives.

What does the death and resurrection of Christ mean? We need the whole of the New Testament to answer that question, but think here of the declaration in 2 Timothy 1:10. The verse speaks of Jesus Christ coming into the world and describes His work in these terms:

> '... the appearing of our Saviour Christ Jesus, who abolished death and brought life and immortality to light through the gospel.'

What a magnificent statement that is regarding the life, death and resurrection of Jesus! He has abolished death, that is, cancelled it out as a tyrannical force and power over human life and experience, and He has brought into evidence, for our possession, life that is free from inherent decay. Think also of 1 Peter 1:3

> 'Blessed be the God and Father of our Lord Jesus Christ! By His great mercy we have been born anew to a living hope through the resurrection of Jesus Christ from the dead.'

Death is conquered and abolished! Those who believe in the name of Jesus Christ unto salvation are brought by the resurrection into newness of life. If we pursued this theme we could go through the New Testament showing over and over again that a Christian is spoken of as one who is alive from the dead.

Paul affirms this in Romans 6:4,6, speaking of those who have been justified by faith and so united to Christ.

> 'We were buried therefore with Him (Christ) by baptism into death, so that (just) as Christ was

raised from the dead by the glory of the Father, (even so) we too might walk in newness of life.
We know that our old self (the person we once were by nature) was crucified with Him so that ... we might no longer be enslaved to sin.'

Read the whole of Romans 6:1-14; read it over and over again until the gospel of the resurrection thrills you with possibilities.

The Bible declares that 'if any one is in Christ he is a new creation' (2 Corinthians 5:17). If we have come to Christ and claimed Him as Saviour this is what has happened to us. We have been put to death and have been raised in newness of life. The Bible says we are new creatures, not a reformed creature, not a renovated second-hand person, but a new creation altogether, raised from the dead in the resurrection of Jesus Christ.

And the presence of Jesus Christ alive from the dead in the midst of His disciples is the assured gospel promise of victory over every power that can ever assail a human life. Just as Jesus Christ's death was the answer to our sins, so His resurrection is the answer to our defeat and to our bondage to sin. Jesus Christ, alive from the dead, has demonstrated that He is total and absolute Victor, and the victory He won is given to us who believe. The sins of pride and passion, the habits of youth and of old age, the defects of character, the fears of our hearts, the bondage, the brokenness, the limitation of life, everything that can dog us and make us so miserable with regard to the poverty of our Christian lives, all these things are overcome; and the proof, the guarantee, is Christ alive from the dead.

That is the message of the resurrection. Sin is overcome. Death is overcome. Hell is overcome. Satan is overcome. Men are overcome. Circumstances are overcome. Christ is risen from the dead.

This has all to do with facts. It is, first of all, a fact of history that cannot be denied. One of the most thoroughly attested happenings this world has ever known is the bodily resurrection of our Lord and Saviour Jesus Christ. The removal of the body could not have been the work of the disciples: they did not expect it, and the Jews, in any case, prevented it with the guard over the grave. The removal of the body could not have been the work of the Pharisees, because that was the last thing in the world they wanted to happen. If they had been in possession of the body all they needed to do in the early days of the Christian church was to produce the corpse and the Christian message would have collapsed. But they did not, because they could not.

I doubt if there are many events with more proof than the resurrection. Consider those who witnessed Christ alive from the dead. Paul speaks of a list of witnesses mentioning individual names and also five hundred gathering at one time. They could not all have been hallucinating (1 Corinthians 15:3-8). Think of doubting Thomas. What a dogged character he was. 'Except I see, except I touch, I will not believe.' And the risen Lord of glory came down to his level and said, 'Well, Thomas, touch, and be not faithless but believing.' Think of Peter the failure, who denied his Lord. No mere wishful thinking could have restored and transformed him. Another proof is the transformation of the disciples from being cowards to men of courage. How do you think they could walk into the Roman arenas and watch the lions being let out of the cages to come and tear them apart? Would they do that for a mere imagination? Never! Remember Stephen, the first martyr, being murdered, and how he looked up and saw Jesus alive from the dead (Acts 7:55). Think of Saul of Tarsus (who became Paul, the great apostle), a man who was at first so antagonistic to the faith, being intellectually persuaded, emotionally grasped, and his will surrendered to the gospel. Why? He met Jesus alive from the dead (Acts 9:4,5).

If only we had eyes able to see, we too would see Jesus Christ right here alive from the dead. He would come to us and He would show His hands and His feet, and He would say, 'This was for you, and having died for you, I have come now alive from the dead in all the glory of My victory over sin and Satan, over death and hell, to give all that to you, to be your possession for time and for eternity'.

It is both a fact of history and a fact of faith. Here is the seal, the guarantee that all the work of the atonement had been accepted. Think of this in terms of the Day of Atonement in the Old Testament, when the High Priest, with the blood of sacrifice, entered into the holiest place of the Tabernacle. At the foot of his robes there were little bells, so that as he moved round in the semi-darkness of the Holy Shrine to sprinkle the blood of the sacrifice on the Mercy Seat, the people might hear the tinkling of the bells and would know that he was still alive. He was, as their representative, in the presence of God, and still alive. The people waited, and when the High Priest came back out of that holy place of the Tabernacle with empty hands, the blood of the sacrifice being left, as it were, in the presence of God, the people knew that atonement had been made. Their God had accepted them. There was peace. That is what the resurrection declares, for Christ comes forth alive from the dead to give us the guarantee that the work of atonement for sin has been accomplished.

But it is not only the work of atonement He declares; He comes from the dead to give us the guarantee of His victory over every power that would ever blight our human lives. Let it be said as clearly as possible, especially to younger people, that there is not a sin, a temptation, a power, a passion that can ever enter into your life but it has to bow to the authority of Jesus Christ, risen victorious from the grave. When Jesus rose from the dead, He came to His disciples to persuade them that all He had done was given to them to be made a fact of their own experience. Can we not imagine Jesus speaking to His disciples and saying to them, 'My children, My victory over sin, My victory over death, My victory over the grave, My victory over hell, My victory over the powers of darkness, My victory over time, My victory over history, My victory over men, My victory over devils, *all of it* I give to you'. You can almost imagine His disciples saying, 'Lord, does that mean we do not need to be defeated by anything or anybody?' And Jesus would have said, 'Exactly! Whatever men do to you, whatever may happen, whatever you may meet, remember My victory is yours, and lo, I am with you always.'

When that message finally dawned upon the disciples nothing could hold them back, and they went out and suffered, bled and died, but they could not be stopped, because they knew that the great Saviour Jesus Christ, risen victorious from the grave, was with them, and that from then right on to the end He would lead them along in the procession of His triumph. Put it very simply. If this risen Christ, alive for evermore, victorious over all in earth and in hell, is *your* Saviour, then *you* cannot be beaten, *you* cannot lose, *you* cannot be turned back.

He is Lord. When we go out into life, He goes with us. Down through the years He is with us and all His triumph is ours. That is the message of the resurrection.

CHAPTER SEVEN

CHRIST ASCENDED

In order to understand the statement, 'He ascended into heaven, and sitteth on the right hand of God the Father Almighty,' we must go to the categorical affirmations of Holy Scripture. In all our studying, as in all our preaching, we must learn to bring ourselves to the Word of God, to anchor ourselves in the Word of God, to be taught by the Word of God, to stay with the Word of God, and to go back over and over again to the same Word of God, which is living and powerful and able to make us wise unto salvation.

In dealing with matters of biblical truth a threefold division or aspect is discernible. Firstly there are the facts of history as recorded and testified to by Holy Scripture. The Christian gospel is not fiction, but has to do with historical facts. We are declaring things that happened, things that were not done in a corner, things that can bear scrutiny and examination. Next we have the theology, the setting forth of the significance of the historical facts, explained, interpreted and expounded by and in the Scriptures. We start with the facts and then the Bible tells us what these facts mean in relation to God. Finally we have the application of that theology to personal experience, so that by faith, not by intellect, nor by emotion, we live in and by the power of the saving truth of God.

In that threefold framework the heart is theology, the explanation, the exposition of the truth, because we cannot base our lives on something that we do not understand. Therefore we approach our subject with the simple question, 'What does it mean when the Christian says concerning Jesus Christ, who was crucified, dead and buried and who rose the third day, that He ascended into heaven, and sits on the right hand of God the Father Almighty?'

You do not sit down and relax until your necessary work is finished. That is a fundamental precept of most housewives, and it should be the basic attitude of all people to their essential work. When Christ sat down at the right hand of the throne of God, His work was finished. There was nothing else to be done and the final issue of the work was beyond doubt.

> 'When Christ had offered for all time a single sacrifice for sins, He sat down at the right hand of God' (Hebrews 10:12).

Notice how a single verse of Scripture counters a fundamental concept of the Roman Catholic Mass, which professes to re-enact, or to repeat, the sacrifice of Christ: the idea being that the word of the priest transforms the bread and wine into the very body and blood of Jesus Christ, so that the Son of God is really crucified afresh. That cannot be. This man Jesus, after He had offered one full and perfect sacrifice for sins forever, never needing to be repeated, sat down at the right hand of God, and is waiting in expectation until the fruit of His work is proved and demonstrated in history and all His enemies are made His footstool.

This does not mean that Jesus is no longer active, but it does show that His ascension into heaven and His being seated at the right hand of God the Father Almighty is the climax of the whole of His life and work. It is the seventh and final 'peak point' in the experience of our Lord and Saviour Jesus Christ: His birth, His baptism, His temptation, His transfiguration, His crucifixion, His resurrection and His ascension. Here is the climax of it all. He came, He lived, He died, He rose, He ascended into the presence of the glory of the Father, having obtained eternal redemption for us (Hebrews 9:12). In the Acts of the Apostles we find that there runs through all the preaching of the early apostles a tremendous thrill of joy because of all that Christ had accomplished. They knew there was no doubt about the final issues. All that Christ had accomplished in His life, death, resurrection and ascension was being sent down amongst men in and by the power of the Holy Ghost. This is what made the disciples thrill with joy. This is what made them go out and preach the gospel, not counting the cost: Jesus, far from being dead and gone, was alive, and from the throne of His glory was working amongst men in power. If we really believe this we would not be such dull Christians.

We must ask a question here. If Jesus rose bodily from the grave, where is He? His was not a spiritual or a ghostly resurrection, because He said, 'Touch Me and see; a ghost does not have flesh and bones' (Luke 24:36-43 N.I.V.). If He rose bodily from the grave, where then is that true and recognisable man whose name is Jesus? Where is He now and what is He doing? These are important questions. We know from Scripture that when Jesus rose again from the dead, He rose a true man in a bodily resurrection, and yet He was free from all the limitations of a materialistic universe. He appeared amongst His disciples and disappeared again at will. He appeared in one place, and then, not allowing enough time for normal travel, appeared in another place to a different group of disciples. He came among His disciples through closed doors. That is all very wonderful and yet it has limitations because it seems He could still be in only one place at one time. Imagine how the disciples would want to keep him, as Mary did, when she went to the sepulchre. In the garden, finally recognising Christ, she went to cling to Him, as if to say,

'Jesus, don't go away again.' He said, 'Do not hold Me, for I am not yet ascended to the Father; but go to My brethren and say to them I am ascending to My Father and your Father, to My God and your God' (John 20:17).

In His ascension, far from leaving them in the lurch, Jesus was establishing a fuller and more permanent relationship, in which two things are gloriously true. The first is expressed in the words Jesus spoke to His disciples after the resurrection and before the ascension, 'Lo, I am with you always' (Matthew 28:20). That means exactly what it says! Jesus said, 'Grasp this fact. I am not staying with you physically or visibly. But I am with you always.' The second thing is that He will be with the Father. The disciples, always being apt to ask questions, might well have said, 'But where exactly will You be?' If He is at the right hand of God the Father Almighty, how can He be *here* with us and *there* with God? If He is there with God in what sense is He here with us?

The most straightforward historical record of the ascension is found in Acts 1:8-11, a passage that tells of the disciples staring up into the heavens as Jesus was taken from their sight. This is the kind of statement that exasperates modern theologians and philosophers and others who seem to find it impossible to accept in any sense that heaven is 'up there'. Some even seem to speak of heaven as being 'down here'. If *this* is heaven, God help us! God the Holy Ghost, who inspired the writers of the Scripture record, was accurate in His terminology. When we read of Jesus going up into heaven and a cloud receiving Him, I cannot forbear commenting on the observation of the heavenly messengers when they said, 'Why do you stand looking up into heaven?' If this had happened to any of us, there is no doubt at all we would have been open-mouthed in astonishment, gazing up to the clouds. There are still some things in human experience that make us gape in astonishment, things which are beyond our comprehension, but are still true.

The disciples were looking up to heaven. That is the Spirit-given description of the scene. Now God has to use language because that is the vehicle by which He can communicate the truth to us, and He can only use language that we understand. When He speaks about Christ being taken *up* into heaven, He is indicating a realm that is above, outside and beyond what we know as this world. This is important. We must never limit the possibilities of experience to what *we* know *now*. That would be sheer conceit. Some say they just cannot understand this idea of being taken up into heaven. Other people say it is because they are scientifically trained that they cannot believe it. Some say that unless it can be proved and demonstrated they will not believe it. But human blindness, incapacity and limitation do not cancel out reality: that would be to take the mighty God and reduce Him to our own puny size.

It is not permissible to say that a thing cannot be, simply because it is beyond what we can understand. Some people can be dogged and virtually unmoveable in their ignorance. But these disciples were there when Christ ascended. They saw it, they watched it, and they proved the power of it. We must believe their testimony. The actual writer of the story was Luke, a scientific medical man who made it his business to get his facts right. They were looking up, to a realm that was above, outside and beyond what we know as 'this world'. Is it not true to say there was a time when all the present-day talk of millions and millions of miles of space travel would have been absolutely beyond our grasp? People used to ridicule the idea of man landing on the moon. That was regarded as fiction. Now it has happened. In a very real sense men are only now slowly emerging from an appalling ignorance of the real facts of life and of experience.

I, for one, do not find any difficulty whatever in thinking of Him 'up there'. I do not interpret that purely in terms of the world as we presently know it. Yet it is real and it must be real, because if it is not real, where is this Jesus who has a 'real' resurrection body and who assured the disciples it was so when He said, 'Touch Me and see. A ghost does not have flesh and bone?' One of the 'baptisms' that we need in this generation is a baptism of reality concerning things that are unseen, things that cannot be tabulated and computerised.

We must never presume to say that what we mean here by the ascension of Jesus Christ into the presence of God, and His being seated at the right hand of God the Father Almighty, is scientifically impossible. The historical record states that a cloud received Him out of their sight. It does not say He just disappeared. What is this 'cloud' that received and enveloped the ascending Jesus? Some say that we need not pin-point the exact words of Scripture. But when we are writing an important letter we choose our words carefully so that the exact meaning will be communicated. We must not digress into a dissertation on the verbal inspiration of Holy Scripture, but that is the position we hold.

A cloud received Him out of their sight. What Bible stories or what pictures are evoked by the thought of the cloud? There was a cloud at the top of Mount Sinai when Moses went up the mountain to the presence of God to receive the commandments (Exodus 19:9). When the High Priest of Israel went into the Tabernacle in the wilderness on the Day of Atonement was there not a significant sign? Did not a cloud come down (Leviticus 16:1,2)? And the people knew by this visible sign, whose significance they could understand, that their high priestly representative was in the presence of the glory of God. There was a cloud which led the Israelites on their journeys and that cloud reassured them that their God was with them and amongst them (Exodus 13:21). Was there not the same cloud on the Mount of Transfiguration when Peter, James and John were astonished by the brightness of glory? Then the cloud disappeared, and they saw no man save Jesus only (Matthew 17:5-8). The cloud represents and speaks to us of the presence of God, and when the cloud received Jesus out of their sight, the disciples knew what had happened. He had passed from their sight into the presence of the glory of God. They remembered His prayer, 'Now, Father, glorify thou Me in Thy own presence with the glory which I had with Thee before the world was made' (John 17:5).

The ascension speaks first of all of the heavenly priesthood of Christ. A priest is one who entered into the presence of God and acted there on behalf of the people.

> 'Seeing then that we have a great high priest, that is passed into the heavens, Jesus the Son of God, let us hold fast our profession (of faith)' (Hebrews 4:14 AV).

It is not a mere legal representative that we have, someone so high and mighty that He does not understand what we really think and feel. Think of the temptations and struggles of life as we read Scripture:

> 'For we have not a high priest who is unable to sympathise with our weaknesses, but one who in every respect has been tempted as we are, yet without sinning. Let us then with confidence draw near to the throne of grace, that we may receive mercy and find grace to help in time of need' (Hebrews 4:15,16).

'He holds His priesthood permanently, because He continues for ever. Consequently He is able for all time to save those who draw near to God through Him, since He always lives to make intercession for them' (Hebrews 7:24,25).

Think of the paraphrase of Romans 8:34-39,

'The Saviour died, but rose again
Triumphant from the grave;
And pleads our cause at God's right hand,
Omnipotent to save.'

If you ever feel that no-one understands you, you are wrong. All other human friends may fail, but not Jesus. If you ever feel that there is no one prepared to stand by you, to take your side, and to speak on your behalf, you are wrong. There is Jesus Christ your great High Priest who not only understands you but also feels with you and for you. When great waves of feeling come over you, He shares and feels all of it with you. When your whole inner being seems to be overwhelmed and crushed, and the tears seem to be squeezed out of your eyes, He is weeping with you. He stands in the presence of God, saying, 'Father Almighty, remember that one. Look down upon that one.'

That is what the ascension means: Jesus in the presence of God on our behalf.

'Though now ascended up on high,
He bends on earth a brother's eye;
Partaker of the human name,
He knows the frailty of our frame.

'In every pang that rends the heart
The Man of sorrows had a part;
He sympathises with our grief,
And to the sufferer sends relief' (Scottish Paraphrases 58).

It is not a mere angel who is in the presence of God on our behalf. It is no mere legal representative but the One who shared our humanity, died for our salvation and who now sits by sovereign entitlement at the right hand of God the Father Almighty.

> 'Now the point in what we are saying is this: we have such an high priest, one who is seated at the right hand of the throne of the Majesty in heaven' (Hebrews 8:1).

> 'Christ being come an high priest of good things to come, by a greater and more perfect tabernacle, not made with hands, that is to say, not of this (earthly) building; neither by the blood of goats and calves, but by His own blood He entered in once (for all) into the holy place (into the very presence of God), having obtained eternal (unchanging and unchangeable) redemption for us' (Hebrews 9:11,12 AV).

It is a salvation that cannot be taken away. That is why the early martyrs of the Christian church were able to die. Take my goods, my honour, my children, my wife, my life itself; no-one can take from me that which Christ has obtained on my behalf. Nor can I be taken from Christ.

> 'Who then can e'er divide us more
> from Jesus and His love,
> Or break the sacred chain that binds
> the earth to heav'n above?' (Scottish Paraphrases 48).

Nothing! No one!

> 'For Christ has entered, not into a sanctuary made with hands, a copy of the true one, but into heaven itself, now to appear in the presence of God on our behalf' (Hebrews 9:24).

'But when Christ had offered for all time a single sacrifice for sins (never to be repeated), He sat down at the right hand of God, then to wait until His enemies should be made a stool for His feet' (Hebrews 10:12,13).

'What then shall we say to this? If God is for us, who is against us? He who did not spare His own Son but gave Him up for us all, will He not also give us all things with Him? Who shall bring any charge against God's elect? It is God who justifies; who is to condemn? Is it Christ Jesus who died, yes, who was raised from the dead, who is at the right hand of God, who indeed intercedes for us?' (Romans 8:31-34).

Shall Christ condemn us, He who is even now at the right hand of God, who also makes intercession for us? We know how deeply we are moved when someone says to us, 'I have been praying every day for you.' Christ's intercession far exceeds that, for in the world of eternity there are no 'days'; there is no past, present or future. And we have One who says to us, 'My child, did you know that all the time, unbroken, unwearied, never misdirected, never misunderstanding, never changing, I speak on your behalf at the throne of God's power and grace?'

Turn to the first epistle of John. The first chapter declares that if we say we have no sin we deceive ourselves, and the truth is not in us. But if we confess our sins, He is faithful and just to forgive, and to cleanse us from all unrighteousness (1 John 1:8,9). John goes on to say:

'My little children, I am writing this to you so that you may not sin; but if anyone does sin, we have an advocate with the Father, Jesus Christ the righteous (one)' (1 John 2:1).

In the very moment of our sinning, He pleads in the presence of God, not our innocence, because that would be a lie, but over against our sin He places the eternal merit of His death on the cross to pay the price of our sin. Put it like this: in the very moment of our sinning, that blessed voice, in the presence of the great white throne of God, says, 'Father, that sin is paid for.' That is wonderful and astonishing! He pleads our cause at God's right hand, omnipotent to save.

This Jesus, ascended to the right hand of the Father, this Jesus touched with the feeling of our infirmities, is our advocate in the presence of God. Among His many activities is this: He takes our poor stumbling prayers, and He presents them *in His own name* as His own, to the Father, and they are accepted for Jesus' sake. That is what we mean when we finish off our prayers, 'For Jesus' sake,' or 'In Jesus' name.' Just as you come to the end of your personal prayers, perhaps before you lie down to sleep, you can imagine the voice of the Father Almighty from the throne saying, 'Whose prayer is this? Who presents this petition?' The voice that answers is the voice of Jesus, your great High Priest. 'This prayer is in My name.'

Another thing that the ascension of Christ and His sitting down at God's right hand speaks of is the giving of the Holy Spirit.

> 'Now this He said about the Spirit, which those who believed in Him were to receive; for as yet the Spirit had not been given, because Jesus was not yet glorified' (John 7:39).

But now He has ascended into the glory of the Father and, in faithfulness to His promise, the Father, through the Son, sends the Holy Spirit down to the believing men and women who have put their trust in Jesus Christ. Listen to the Word of God:

'And while staying with them He charged them not to depart from Jerusalem, but to wait for the promise of the Father, which He said, "you heard from Me" ' (Acts 1:4).

'You shall receive power when the Holy Spirit has come upon you; and you shall be My witnesses in Jerusalem and in all Judea and Samaria and to the end of the earth' (Acts 1:8).

'Being therefore exalted at the right hand of God, and having received from the Father the promise of the Holy Spirit, He has poured out this which you see and hear' (Acts 2:33).

The power of the Holy Ghost, who has all the attributes of the mighty God of eternity, comes down not only to touch and to hold, but to indwell the lives of believing men and women, to set them afire with the life of God, sending them out like blazing spiritual coals to set the whole world on fire. Jesus, having finished His work, entered into the presence of the Father, claiming from the Father, not for Himself but for you and me who believe in His name, the promise of the life and the power of His Holy Spirit. That Spirit sent down to us causes us to be born again and to be partakers of the very life of God.

This Holy Spirit is the Spirit of truth, leading us into the truth. He is the Spirit of holiness, convicting us of our sin, and clearing up the tangled mess of our lives, pushing out increasingly that which is rubble and replacing it with pure qualities that are eternal. The Holy Spirit is the Spirit of power. Let it be said clearly that no Christian can ever say, 'I cannot do what I should,' because God, in all His grace and glory and power, dwells in the heart of every believer by the Holy

Spirit. When we listen to the preaching of the gospel, when we hear the Word of God being taught to us, when we become aware of our hunger for a Saviour, when we open our hearts and we receive Christ as our Saviour, in that very moment we receive the gift of the Holy Spirit sent down from Heaven.

God the Father, through the Son, by the Holy Spirit leads us on, teaches us and transforms us in this salvation. In John 14:16 Jesus promised His disciples that after His death the Father would send them another Counsellor to be with them and in them for ever.

'I will pray the Father, and He will give you another Counsellor.'

The word 'Counsellor' or 'Comforter' is 'paraclete', which is a Greek word meaning or signifying one called alongside to help. That same word 'paraclete' is translated in the first epistle of John 'advocate' (1 John 2:1). We have two advocates. We have one 'up there' speaking our cause in the presence of God, and we have the other here, speaking God's cause within our hearts and our lives. It is marvellous.

'... another Counsellor to be with you for ever, even the Spirit of truth, whom the world cannot receive, because it neither sees Him nor knows Him; you know Him, for He dwells with you, and *will be in you*' (John 14:16,17).

It is perhaps childish to think in this way, but sometimes when we are on our own, we could almost say, 'Lord, are You there?' The Holy Spirit bears witness in our spirits that we are in fact born of God and that God is with us. When we pray we begin to say, 'Father', and we know that it is true (Romans 8:15,16).

This Guide and Teacher is our inseparable companion. Wherever we are, Jesus, risen, ascended and glorified is there, for He is our life. At the same time, in the sovereignty of His glory and in the limitlessness of His power, He is pleading our cause every moment in God's presence. Before we are aware of the need, He has already spoken it in the presence of the Father.

The last emphasis of the ascension concerns the triumph of Christ the King, for God has exalted Him and given Him a name that is above every name, that at the name of Jesus every knee should bow. That conquering One is our Saviour, our Shepherd, our Keeper, our Friend, our Counsellor, our Guide, our Lover in tenderness and faithfulness, surpassing any other love that can ever be known. This is the One who says:

'I have said this to you, that in Me you may have peace. In the world you have tribulation; but be of good cheer, I have overcome the world' (John 16:33).

'Little children, you are of God, and have overcome them; for He who is in you is greater than he who is in the world' (1 John 4:4).

This is how He sent His disciples out:

'All authority in heaven and earth has been given to Me. Go therefore and make disciples of all nations' (Matthew 28:18ff).

We go out into the world with this assurance:

'God exalted Him at His right hand as Leader and Saviour, to give repentance to Israel and forgiveness of sins' (Acts 5:31).

To be a Christian in the light of all this is to go out with the unmistakable and undeniable knowledge that Jesus is in our hearts to plead God's cause and work it out there. And that same Jesus is in heaven to plead our cause at God's right hand, omnipotent to save and keep.

CHAPTER EIGHT

CHRIST RETURNING

The theme of the Second Coming of Christ is stated in the words of the Creed to the effect that from His place at the right hand of God the Father Almighty, Jesus Christ shall come to judge the living (the quick) and the dead. There are many, including scholarly theologians, who seek to spiritualise or explain away this doctrine of the personal return of the Lord Jesus Christ. Some say that Christ comes again in the giving of the Spirit, or when men are brought to faith, or in the fellowship of the saints when they are gathered together. But that is not what the Bible says.

In the Acts of the Apostles we read:

> 'Men of Galilee, why do you stand looking into heaven? This Jesus, who was taken up from you into heaven, will come in the same way as you saw Him go into heaven' (Acts 1:11).

Just as He left this world and ascended to the Father, in like manner this same Jesus shall return again, before the astonished eyes of the population of the whole world. This same Jesus, risen from the dead in a bodily resurrection and alive for evermore, a glorified man in heaven, shall return. *This same Jesus*, not a ghost, nor a memory, nor an influence; this real identifiable, recognisable Jesus shall come again.

> 'For this we declare to you by the word of the Lord, that we who are alive, who are left until the coming of the Lord, shall not precede those who have fallen asleep. *For the Lord Himself* will descend from heaven with a cry of command, with the archangel's call, and with the sound of the trumpet of God. And the dead in

Christ will rise first; then we who are alive, who are left, shall be caught up together with them in the clouds to meet the Lord in the air; and so we shall always be with the Lord' (1 Thessalonians 4:15-17).

Notice again that the Word says, the Lord *Himself* shall descend from heaven.

When we speak of the Second Coming of Christ, we must be quite clear in our minds that we are speaking of the personal return of our Lord and Saviour Jesus Christ, recognisable to our eyes whether we be people of faith or people of unbelief. Every eye shall see Him (Revelation 1:7) in the magnificence of His glory. His coming marks the final consummation of history as we know it, and brings us to the point of the establishment of the eternal kingdom of God with a new heaven and a new earth (whatever that may mean), a completely new order of existence from which sin and its fruits are excluded for ever.

The return of Jesus Christ is a doctrine, so I am told, that is referred to in Scripture over three hundred times, and that works out at an average of once every thirteen verses of the New Testament. This fact of Christ's return in glory to confront men, and to bring them to judgment, is spoken of many times, whereas the Lord's Supper is referred to only a few times. This is some indication of the earnestness with which we must address ourselves to this doctrine. It is a fact of future history that we must come to grips with, no matter how much men try to deny it.

Jesus said to the disciples:

'And when I go and prepare a place for you, I will come again and will take you to Myself, that where I am you may be also' (John 14:3).

If He did not mean that He would come again, why

did He say He would? If He meant some vague, nebulous, spiritual application, why did He not say so? The disciples would certainly understand the words in a real, personal sense. Jesus told His persecutors that He would return:

> 'Hereafter you will see the Son of man... coming on the clouds of heaven' (Matthew 26:64).

As we have already noted the messengers of God sent from heaven said it at the time of the ascension.

Paul in his epistles said it:

> 'For the Lord Himself will descend from heaven with a cry of command' (1 Thessalonians 4:16).
> 'Now concerning the coming of our Lord Jesus Christ and our assembling to meet Him, we beg you, brethren, not to be quickly shaken in mind or excited, either by spirit or word, or by letter purporting to be from us, to the effect that the day of the Lord has come' (2 Thessalonians 2:1-2).

The Book of Revelation says it:

> 'He is coming with the clouds, and every eye will see Him' (1:7).
> 'Behold I am coming soon' (22:7).

The Christian church right down through its history has affirmed the fact, in creed and in action. Every time we gather at the Lord's table we declare the Lord's death, not in perpetuity, but 'until He come'. There will be a time when we sit at the communion table for the last time.

The New Testament is quite clear about this doctrine. It declares the fact that Jesus Christ will return, personally, and in glory; and we are given many vivid illustrations of the nature of His coming.

Scripture applies the fact of the Second Coming of Christ in terms of moral and spiritual challenge. One note seems to recur: the return of the Lord Jesus Christ is the end of all we call history, the end of this world as we know it, the end of earthly human experience. There may well be some who read these words who will not, as we assume, live out the rest of their alloted span. Quite apart from considerations of health or accident, shall we reach thirty, forty, fifty, sixty years of age? Only if the Lord Jesus Christ does not return before then. This is the fact that Scripture affirms three hundred times over, saying that there is an end, a consummation, a curtain-call. This is the point at which there takes place that final and eternal separation between those who are Christ's through faith, and those who are not Christ's because they have never received Him, never acknowledged Him and never bowed to Him, however much they may have known of the theory of salvation or the practice of religion.

Christ is coming again, and when the author walks on to the stage the play is finished. The time will come when the Lord Jesus Christ, with the voice of the archangel and the trumpet of God sounding in glorious triumph, will come on to the stage of human history, and in so doing will create a consternation of delight and confusion. There will be those who will rejoice to see Him. There will also be those who, seeing Him more clearly than they have ever been prepared to see Him in all their earthly existence, will confirm that they hate this Jesus and resent His every claim as Saviour and Lord, even as they stand face to face with Him. So the great gulf is fixed in the kingdom that is eternal. Those that are His are gathered in, the door is shut, and the rest are outside.

This is the first emphasis of the Second Coming. It tells us (and this is something that may mean more to younger people than older ones) that history is going somewhere. One trouble with our present age is that we are dealing with a generation that seems to have nothing to aim for. There is no objective, no bright shining target for men and women to fix their sights on. There is a spirit of pessimism today, and it has seeped into the fibre of all age groups, including the younger generation. It stems from the concept of history as being nothing, not going anywhere, with nowhere to reach, no consummation, nothing! People think of history and experience as being a treadmill of repetition, and they feel (and feelings are important) as if life and experience are things that just spin into nothingness, with a gradual slowing down and disintegration. What emptiness! What futility! What absence of any sense of destiny!

In one sense we can understand young people wanting to take drugs and go on a 'trip' when they find themselves in a generation like this. Where are we going? It seems the answer is - nowhere! That is what the world says, and the church seems to echo it, because some of the theologians of the church have brought about a denial of the fundamental facts of the Christian faith. I do not altogether blame people for their attitudes but I grieve for them. When we demolish the Christian concept of history, when we rob the human situation of the final glorious objective and consummation in the coming of Jesus Christ, there is nothing left.

Consider some words from three different historians of considerable reputation. G.N. Clark, a Cambridge historian, says:

> 'There is no secret plan, there is no plan in history to be discovered. I do not believe that any future consummation could make sense of the irrationality of the ages.'

What can that man tell people to live for? He says there is no purpose or point. Another famous historian, H.A.L. Fisher, whose history of Europe used to be a standard university text-book says:

> 'Men far wiser than I am have discovered or discerned in history a plot, a rhythm, a pre-determined plan, but I can see only one emergency following another, wave upon wave.'

Another, Andre Maurois, declares:

> 'The universe is indifferent. Who created it? Why are we here on this puny mud-heap, spinning in infinite space? I have not the slightest idea and am convinced that no one else has the slightest idea.'

This is the philosophy of life that has blighted our generation. This is the emptiness that has dominated the thinking, feeling, desiring, hoping and longing of a whole age. People have heard countless voices saying to them that there is nothing now and nothing to come. You can understand why people try to escape, and if in the process they kill themselves, what does it really matter, because according to this view there is nothing now, and there is nothing to come. This is the reason why men and women of all ages, of all social backgrounds, of every intellectual and artistic capacity, are groping for 'experiences' in life, experimenting with anything and everything, even the most gross and perverted things. They try this, that and the other thing, in the hope that they might find something that will make life coherent, understandable and satisfying, something that will give direction, dynamic and purpose.

Over against this ghastly emptiness we must place the teaching of Scripture with regard to the personal return of our Lord and Saviour Jesus Christ. Think first of 2 Peter 3:1-14. The essence of this epistle, which is one of the latest in the New Testament, is a rebuke to those who were saying that because the Lord's return had been delayed it was not going to happen. It affirms quite categorically that the day of the Lord will come (2 Peter 3:10). There is no suggestion whatever of history's being an undulating continuance, going on and on, world without end. Far less is there any suggestion in the passage, or anywhere else in the Bible, of the slow but sure emerging of some human Utopia, some human kingdom of God upon the earth, brought about by a gradual Christianisation of society. (Neither is there any indication of a coming Utopia in our daily newspapers.) God the Holy Spirit, through the words of the apostle Peter, is pointing out the mingling of cause and effect, the interaction of one nation's affairs with another's, with groups of nations over against groups of nations, and the alliances ever changing. We do well to recall that in the last war Russia was on our side. Whose side will the various nations and powers be on in the next war? What a strange, tangled skein world history is! So many things are inexplicable to our limited minds, and utterly beyond us.

The Word of God points right through all the tortuous wanderings of history to a fixed objective, the Coming of the Lord. This chapter in 2 Peter pictures all the different strands of history gradually coming together and moving towards one climactic point, that point being reached, not in universal peace, but in an almighty explosion. In the Gospels we are told that the 'day of the Lord' will come, as a thief in the night, taking people unawares. Peter was well aware of the words of Jesus and refers to them, but goes on to say:

> 'The day of the Lord will come like a thief, and then the heavens will pass away with a loud noise, and the elements will be dissolved with fire, and the earth and the works that are upon it will be burned up. Since all these things are thus to be dissolved, what sort of persons ought

you to be ...?' (2 Peter 3:10,11).

That is a frightening concept: dissolution! People say we cannot take it to mean literally what it says. What else does it mean? The Bible means what it says. In these circumstances we are to be:

> 'Waiting for and hastening (earnestly desiring) the coming of the day of God, because of which the heavens will be kindled and dissolved, and the elements will melt with fire' (2 Peter 3:12).

It would be easy to be a scaremonger with regard to nuclear explosions, but it may well be that we have only come to the initial stage of discovering destructive power. The day may not be far hence when our present nuclear power will fade into nothing compared to power such as this. Read in newspapers or watch on television the stories of man-made rockets, satellites and moon platforms. The talk is of going further and further, growing greater and greater, ruling vaster and vaster territory, always with the thought of having the power to control and to destroy the enemy. It is frightening.

Peter, writing by the inspiration of the Holy Spirit, visualises history coming to a climactic point of immense disturbance, disruption and dissolution, but not issuing in nothingness for:

> 'According to His promise, we wait for new heavens and a new earth in which righteousness dwells' (2 Peter 3:13).

It is the ushering in of a completely new order of existence. We may find it difficult to conceive of any kind of experience other than the one we know; but that does not mean it cannot exist. Seeing then that all these things shall be dissolved, and seeing that we look for such things to come, what kind of people should we be? We need above all else to be people whose sins are forgiven and who in Jesus Christ are right with God. Further, we need to be people who, being right with God, are set apart from all evil and compromise that would contradict our rightness with God. Do not ignore this. The day of the Lord will come. Feel the throb in the words in the Book of Revelation, 'Behold, I come quickly' (Revelation 22:7 AV).

The best way to think of the coming of the Lord and the climax of history is not in terms of time proceeding towards eternity like a road approaching a T junction. Rather we should think of the world of time and the world of eternity running closely parallel, so very close that the one breaks into the other in a moment, in the twinkling of an eye (1 Corinthians 15:51,52).

Listen to Jesus' words:

> 'And there will be signs in sun and moon and stars, and upon the earth distress of nations in perplexity at the roaring of the sea and the waves, men fainting with fear and with foreboding of what is coming on the world; for the powers of the heavens will be shaken. And then they will see the Son of man coming in a cloud with power and great glory. Now when these things begin to take place, look up and raise your heads, because your redemption is drawing near' (Luke 21:25-28).

> 'Jesus left the temple and was going away, when His disciples came to point out to Him the buildings of the temple (of which they were very proud). But He answered them, "You see all these, do you not (all looking very solid, substantial and enduring)? Truly, I say to you, there will not be left here one stone upon another, that will not be thrown down." '

'As He sat on the Mount of Olives, the disciples came to Him privately, saying, "Tell us (and they asked three clear questions), when will this be, and what will be the sign of Your coming and of the close of the age?"

And Jesus answered them, "Take heed that no one leads you astray. For many will come in My name, saying, 'I am the Christ,' and they will lead many astray. And you will hear of wars and rumours of wars; see that you are not alarmed; for this must take place, but the end is not yet. For nation will rise against nation, and kingdom against kingdom, and there will be famines and earthquakes in various places: all this is but the beginning of the sufferings.

Then they will deliver you up to tribulation, and put you to death; and you will be hated by all nations for My name's sake. And then many will fall away, and betray one another, and hate one another. And may false prophets will arise and lead many astray. And because wickedness is multiplied, most men's love will grow cold. But he who endures to the end will be saved" ' (Matthew 24:1-13).

'For then there will be great tribulation, such as has not been from the beginning of the world until now, no, and never will be' (Matthew 24:21).

'Lo, I have told you beforehand. So, if they say to you, "Lo, he is in the wilderness," do not go out; if they say, "Lo he is in the inner rooms," do not believe it. (You will not need anyone to tell you when Christ comes.) For as the lightning comes from the east and shines as far as the west, so will be the coming of the Son of man.' (It is a moment of brilliance and awareness, quite frightening) (Matthew 24:25-27).

'Immediately after the tribulation of those days the sun will be darkened, and the moon will not give its light, and the stars will fall from heaven, and the powers of the heavens will be shaken; then will appear the sign of the Son of man in heaven, and then all the tribes of the earth will mourn, and they will see the Son of man coming on the clouds of heaven with power and great glory; and He will send out His angels with a loud trumpet call, and they will gather His elect from the four winds, from one end of heaven to the other.

From the fig tree learn its lesson: as soon as its branch becomes tender and puts forth its leaves, you know that summer is near. So also, when you see all these things, you know that He is near, at the very gates' (Matthew 24:29-33).

'But of that day and hour no one knows, not even the angels of heaven, nor the Son, but the Father only. As were the days of Noah, so will be the coming of the Son of man. For as in those days before the flood they were eating and drinking, marrying and giving in marriage, until the day when Noah entered the ark, and they did not know (their danger) until the flood came and swept them all away, so will be the coming of the Son of man. Then two men will be in the field; one (a believer) is taken (into the safety of the presence of the Saviour) and one (an unbeliever) is left. Two women will be grinding at the mill; one is taken and one is left. Watch therefore, for you do not know on what day your Lord is coming. But know this, that if the householder had known in what part of the night the thief was coming, he would have watched and would not have let his house be broken into. Therefore you also must be ready; for the Son of man is coming at an hour you do not expect' (Matthew 24:36-44).

The time is fixed; there is no doubt about that. The time is unexpected; there is no doubt about that either. When the time comes, a great many people will be preoccupied, not necessarily with bad things but with normal things, and they will discover that they have been so preoccupied that they have neglected the salvation of their souls. What do you think your reaction would be if you suddenly became aware, in this lightning flash of revelation of Christ at His coming, that all the Christians you knew were gone, before your very eyes, and you were left? It says in Scripture that the time of Christ's coming is secret, and yet we can read the signs of times. Still, when He comes, it will take men unawares, in a moment, in the twinkling of an eye, at the last trump (1 Corinthians 15:52), for the trumpet shall sound and the Lord Himself will descend from heaven with a shout (1 Thessalonians 4:16). The old redemption hymn says:

> 'When the trumpet of the Lord shall sound,
> And time shall be no more,
> And the morning breaks, eternal, bright and fair:
> When the saved of earth shall gather
> Over on the other shore,
> And the roll is called up yonder, I'll be there'
> (Black).

Are we sure about that?

Are we sure that our sins are forgiven? Are we sure that we have come to Christ to claim Him as Saviour? Are you sure? It may not be long before Christ comes. What a joy it is when some of the older generation want to speak about Jesus. Some of them say, 'When you read the papers, don't you feel that the Lord must come soon?' But people have been saying that for generations. True! Does that not mean that the day must be even nearer now?

What will it mean when Christ comes? Every eye shall see Him. Some will say, 'This is the Jesus who died to save me from my sin. This is the Jesus that I have learned to love. This is the Jesus that I want.' Others will say, 'This is the Jesus I heard about so often, but never responded to. This is the Jesus I have never accepted, never allowed to come into my life.' Do not ignore this: the day of the Lord will come. Be ready, for in such an hour as you think not the Son of man comes. Whatever else you make sure of, make sure that your soul's salvation is safely entrusted to Jesus. And that being so, 'Let your loins be girded (the whole manner of your life disciplined), and your lamps (that is your witness unto the things of Christ) burning, and you yourselves as they that wait for the Lord' (cf. Luke 12:35).

Do you know this verse of Scripture?

'It shall be said in that day, Lo, this is our God; we have waited for Him, and He will save us: this is the Lord; we have waited for Him, we will be glad and rejoice in His salvation' (Isaiah 25:9 AV).

A Bible Class Leader had dealt with the subject of the coming again in glory of our Lord Jesus Christ. At the end of the lesson each was asked to give a considered answer to the question, 'Do you think Jesus will return today?' After due and solemn consideration each replied, 'No, not today'. The class leader quoted the words of Jesus, 'In such an hour as ye think not, the Son of man cometh' (Matthew 24:44 AV).

CHAPTER NINE

THE JUDGMENT

We are required with the help of Holy Scripture to consider the facts of the final judgment. Our Lord Jesus Christ is presently seated at the right hand of God the Father Almighty, from which place He shall come to judge the living and the dead. We must not be afraid to use the words, nor be ashamed of the subjects of hell, damnation, eternal loss and torment. We are dealing with a doctrine that has been neglected by the Christian church possibly more than any other subject. With the theme of final judgment we are brought face to face with the ultimate issues of life and the eternal destiny of our souls, in the presence of God and the blessedness of heaven, or excluded and banished from the presence of God in the eternal torment and loss of hell.

This subject of judgment is no fabrication of a diseased mind. It is a theme that runs right through the Scriptures, which speak over and over again of the day of the Lord, the day of judgment, the day of final separation, as Jesus puts it, between the sheep and the goats. Some of the most solemn, frightening and vivid words concerning judgment and hell come from the lips of none other than our Lord and Saviour Jesus Christ Himself. Therefore we must be honest. We must face up to the truth, not trying to be dramatic (the heart is too burdened for that), not trying to be emotional, and certainly not trying to exaggerate, but facing from the Scriptures the fact of the judgment that is to come. If some of the things we read and learn frighten us, as well they may, then they may bring us to a realistic fear which is the beginning of wisdom (Proverbs 9:10) and this may lead some to salvation.

Consider this passage of Holy Scripture from which, without entering into minute details, we take its stark and significant truth:

> 'Then I saw a great white throne and Him who sat upon it; from His presence earth and sky fled away, and no place was found for them. And I saw the dead, great and small, standing before the throne, and books were opened' (Revelation 20:11,12).

Such a phrase solemnises the heart: the books (the record of all things concerning every man and woman) were opened.

> 'Also another book was opened, which is the book of life. And the dead were judged by what was written in the books, by what they had done. And the sea gave up the dead in it, Death and Hades gave up the dead in them, and all were judged by what they had done. Then Death and Hades were thrown into the lake of fire; ... and if any one's name was not found written in the book of life, he was thrown into the lake of fire' (Revelation 20:12-15).

I have come to the conclusion that one of the great tragedies, and one in which the church of Jesus Christ stands guilty of terrible betrayal of its trust, is that the church in our generation has caused men and women to believe that all will in the end go to heaven. This is not true. Because of our failure to bring home to the souls of men the need to be saved, this false attitude permeates the thinking of our whole generation, not only outside but inside the church. Even amongst converted people there is a refusal, or at least a reluctance, to face up to the fact that men and women can die without Christ and be lost in hell for ever. It is not true that all will in the end go to heaven. Yet many people base their lives upon the false assumption that no matter how they have lived, whether with trust and a love towards Jesus Christ or a contempt and rejection of Him, they will go to heaven when they die. A man may have lived a worldly life excluding Christ, refusing the offer of His great mercy and salvation, having no interest in the Bible, no interest in prayer, no interest in spiritual things, yet when he dies, people say, 'He is at rest now.' It is not true. There is no eternal rest for those who die outside Christ.

The passage from Revelation spoke very clearly of the eternal separation between those who are in Christ, whose names are written in the Lamb's Book of Life and those who are not. This final separation is not a sudden, impromptu judgment. That, in part at least, is the significance of the statement that the books were opened, for God brings to view the undebatable facts of the life choices of every man and woman. There are those who, in the context of the preaching of the Word of God, are made aware of their sin and their need of a Saviour, and they choose Christ. No matter what it costs them they confess Christ and they stand in Him as their Saviour in life, in death and in the judgment. All their hope is built 'on Jesus' blood and righteousness', that is, on His atoning death on the cross. But there are others in the same context, listening to the same preaching, who all through their lives say 'No' to Christ. They do not want a Saviour. They do not want a Master. They do not want a Lord. They do not want spiritual discipleship. They do not want the whole of their lives to be hemmed in, undergirded and governed by this man whose name is Jesus, and they refuse Him. They will not come to Him. They will not repent of their sins. They will not believe. They will not be converted. This is their choice (John 5:40). Jesus said that such persons would die in their sins (John 8:21,24).

The passage from Revelation is very vivid. Think of the financial and fiscal investigations following accusations of fraud. The official investigators come to an office, the books are opened and they are scrutinised in the most minute detail. Nothing escapes the eagle eye. So it is in the day of God's judgment at the great white throne. On the great day of judgment, books are opened and it has all been written, inescapably, incontrovertibly: those who received Christ, who yielded their lives in faith to Him; and those who stood aloof from Christ and trusted in their own righteousness, their own morality or their own church membership to get them to heaven. Those whose names are written in the Lamb's Book of Life are safe in the day of judgment. Whoever is not found in the Lamb's Book of Life will be cast into the lake of fire.

We read in Luke 16:19-31 that, between these two eternal destinies of heaven with its blessedness and hell with its torment, a great gulf is fixed. There is no changing, no repentance, all is fixed; and the fixing is determined, not at the day of judgment, but *now* in this day of grace. Notice that in the passage from Revelation there is no voice at all raised in protest, objection or discussion. It has come to pass that every mouth is stopped and all the world becomes guilty before God (Romans 3:19). The judgment is set.

What is the basis of this judgment? Is it more than simply a judgment in relation to Jesus Christ? We are sometimes asked by those who are really trying to evade the issue (but we can give them credit for genuine concern) about those who have never heard about Jesus Christ. Of course, there is another question here: how does it come about that there are so many people who have never heard of Jesus Christ and His salvation, when there are so many Christians, hale and hearty, free and capable of going out to proclaim His name? But there is an answer in the Scriptures to those who ask concerning those who have never heard the gospel.

Turn to Romans 1:18-20:

'For the wrath of God is revealed from heaven against all ungodliness and wickedness of men who by their wickedness suppress the truth. For what can be known about God is plain to them, because God has shown it to them. Ever since the creation of the world His invisible nature, namely, His eternal power and deity, has been clearly perceived in the things that have been made. So they are without excuse.'

In Romans 2:12ff:

'All who have sinned without the law (that is, outwith the sphere of the law of God, the Word and the teaching of God) will also perish without the law, and all who have sinned under the law (within the sphere of privilege in the law) will be judged by the law. For it is not the hearers of the law who are righteous before God, but the doers of the law who will be justified. When Gentiles who have not the law (who have never heard) do by nature what the law requires, they are a law to themselves (having a Godward moral sense woven deep into the very fabric of their personalities), even though they do not have the law. They show that what the law requires is written on their hearts, while their conscience also bears witness and their conflicting thoughts accuse or perhaps excuse them on that day when, according to my gospel, God judges the secrets of men by Christ Jesus.'

When asked about those who have never heard the gospel we need spend little time debating what is a hypothetical question. We must go to the statement of Scripture, 'Shall not the Judge of all the earth do right?' (Genesis 18:25). We must be so persuaded of the absolute righteousness of Him who sits on the throne that we have no undue anxiety. He who knows the hearts of men, who reads the secrets of the souls of men, shall do right.

Our hearts should be burdened not only for those who have never heard but also for those who have only head-knowledge of the gospel: those who have known the facts of the gospel all the days of their lives, but who, like the rich man in Luke 16:19ff have been so busy living that they have never given a thought on a personal level to the salvation of their souls. Remember Jesus said with regard to Capernaum and similar places He had visited that it would be more tolerable on the day of judgment for Sodom and Gomorrah than for them. There might have been some excuse for those in Sodom and Gomorrah with all the hideous corruption of their dark society, but for those who have known the light and truth of the gospel all the days of their lives, and yet, knowing the facts, have never personally yielded to Jesus Christ in faith, there is no excuse.

Scripture declares that 'it is appointed unto men once to die, but after this the judgment' (Hebrews 9:27 AV). We are left in no doubt: 'We must all appear before the judgment seat of Christ' (2 Corinthians 5:10). If then we believe we have never-dying souls, the most vital question we can ask is, 'Are our souls saved?' Think ahead, how near we cannot predict, to the day when our earthly journey is over and we must die, and, after death, face the judgment. Can we look forward to that day with a measure of equanimity in mind, heart, and spirit, knowing this, sinners that we are, that our sins are forgiven by the merit of the death of Jesus Christ on the cross, so that on that great day as we stand before the throne of God we need not fear the judgment? The rich man in the story had been so busy living that he had never given a thought to the salvation of his soul. Like countless thousands of others, he had just lived, thinking or hoping, if it ever crossed his mind to think, that somehow or other things would work out all right (cf. Luke 16:19-31).

Turn to the words of our Saviour in John 3:16

'God so loved the world, that He gave His only Son, that whoever believes in Him should not perish ....'

Put it as simply as this, Jesus Christ died on the cross to pay the price of our sins so that we would not go to hell. Do we believe that?

'For God sent the Son into the world, not to condemn the world, but that the world might be saved through Him. He who believes in Him (that is, putting all your hope and trust in Him) is not condemned; he who does not believe is condemned already, because he has not believed in the name of the only Son of God. And this is the judgment (this is the verdict), that the light has come into the world, and men loved darkness rather than light, because their deeds were evil' (John 3:17-19).

'He who believes in the Son has eternal life; he who does not obey the Son shall not see life, but the wrath of God rests upon him' (John 3:36).

Do we see what the Bible is saying? Those who have not come to Christ are condemned already. They live here and now in this life with the wrath of God abiding on them, and if they live out their life like that, as the rich man did, they die and they enter eternity with the wrath of God abiding eternally on them, and there is no salvation. They are lost. They are lost eternally.

Have we ever considered why it is that people will not come to Christ, believingly and personally, to receive Him, accept Him and trust Him as their Saviour and Lord? One reason is that the first thing in coming to Christ is to step into the place of being a sinner. Of course, as soon as we begin to say to people that they are sinners and that they need to be saved, they react. They may answer, 'I have done my best. I have worked for the church all my life. I have worked for charity. I have worked for the community, and for my family.' But the Bible says that by the works of the law no flesh shall be justified in God's sight. Think of the hymn 'Rock of Ages:'

> 'Could my zeal no respite know,
> Could my tears for ever flow,
> All for sin could not atone,
> Thou must save, and Thou alone' (Toplady).

Only Jesus can save. That is why we need to say, and to mean it:

> 'Just as I am, without one plea
> But that Thy blood was shed for me,
> And that Thou bidd'st me come to Thee,
> O Lamb of God, I come' (Elliott).

The preacher cannot save anyone. A priest cannot save. A church cannot save. We cannot save ourselves. How could a guilty sinner forgive himself? The sacrament cannot save. But the broken bread and poured out wine speak of the Saviour's dying love, the price that was paid for our salvation on the cross of Calvary. In the sacrament we are shown in dramatic form (it is an action sermon) that the dearly bought salvation that Christ has accomplished is freely offered to us and brought near to us for us to receive by faith. Jesus is the only one who can bring us to God, and keep us in the day of judgment.

Jesus said:

> 'Truly, truly, I say to you, he who hears My word and believes Him who sent Me has eternal life; he does not come into judgment, but has passed from death to life.'

> 'Truly, truly, I say to you, the hour is coming, and now is, when the dead will hear the voice of the Son of God, and those who hear will live. For as the Father has life in Himself, so He has granted the Son also to have life in Himself, and has given Him authority to execute judgment, because He is the Son of man. Do not marvel at this; for the hour is coming when all who are in the tombs will hear His voice and come forth, those who have done good, to the resurrection of life, and those who have done evil, to the resurrection of judgment' (John 5:24-29).

Years ago I spoke to an old lady about salvation. Without a blush of embarrassment (she had been a church woman all her days) she said, 'What I believe is this. When I die and stand before God there will be all the good that I have done and all the bad that I have done, and the good will outweigh the bad, and God will accept me into heaven.' There was a woman staking the whole of her hope of heaven on herself and her own good works. The only hope is Jesus! But the passage just quoted spoke of those who had done good being accepted. Turn to John 6:28,29:

> 'The people said, "What must we do, to be doing the work of God?" Jesus answered them, "This is the work of God, that you believe in Him whom He has sent." '

What is our hope of heaven? What is our security for the day of judgment, when we shall stand before the great white throne of God, and the books are opened? The King Himself shall separate the sheep from the goats (Matthew 25:31ff). He shall say to His own, 'Enter in, beloved, into the presence of My Father.' He shall say to others, 'Depart, ye cursed, into everlasting fire prepared for the Devil and his angels.' Where is our hope resting? Have we a Saviour? It does not matter how well provided we are in respect of this world and its approval; how do we stand with God? How ready are we for the world to come? Are our names written in the Lamb's Book of Life (Revelation 21:27)? Have we in penitence and faith come to Jesus, who alone is able to take away our sins and write our names in that Book of Life? How will be stand on the day of judgment?

> 'While I draw this fleeting breath,
> When mine eyelids close in death,
> When I soar through tracts unknown,
> See Thee on Thy judgment throne,
> Rock of Ages, cleft for me,
> Let me hide myself in Thee' (Toplady).

When the content of this chapter was actually preached on a Communion Sunday, the sermon ended with the following words:

'My dear people, in the interest of the salvation of your souls and your hope on the day of judgment, I bid you come to Christ. Ask Him to be your Saviour, that your sins may be forgiven, and let your whole life be encircled in His saving love. I give you this word as I bid you come, not to the Lord's Table, but to the Lord Jesus Christ Himself:

> "God so loved the world, that He gave His only begotten Son, that whosoever believeth in Him should not perish, but have everlasting life" ' (John 3:16 A.V.).

CHAPTER TEN

THE HOLY SPIRIT (1)

There is something glorious about the sheer brevity of the statement in the Creed, 'I believe in the Holy Ghost'. In our day unfortunately the word 'ghost' has come to indicate something unreal rather than spiritual, something fictitious and even laughable. For this reason we now say, 'I believe in the Holy Spirit,' and affirm that we are dealing with the third person of the eternal Trinity.

Whatever the reason for the reference to the Holy Spirit being confined to a mere six words in the Creed, the person and the work of the Holy Spirit is a subject far beyond the scope of one chapter, or any number of chapters, in a book. There is an extensiveness and limitlessness about the work of the Spirit. He cannot be systematised and must not be restricted. Jesus Himself said that the Spirit blows or moves and works where He wills and no-one can really explain His activity (John 3:8). Those who make arbitrary pronouncements about the activities of the Holy Spirit tend to go beyond what Scripture states clearly, and in fact limit the concept of the Holy Spirit.

At certain times there has been a significant neglect of the Doctrine of the Holy Spirit, and at other times a great deal of confusion resulting from careless talk about the Spirit. It is important that we should consider clearly and carefully what the Bible, Old Testament as well as New Testament, says about the person and work of the Holy Spirit.

If we have come in faith to Jesus Christ and have found in Him salvation, we have been made new creatures with a new life. By the Holy Spirit we are given a new heart, a 'Jesus heart', perfect and right and pure and good. This is the truth of salvation. This is fact whether we are aware of it subjectively or not. We believe that, by the Holy Spirit, the perfect all-sufficient life of the Son of God has in fact been born in us and lives within us. An almighty work of transformation, totally and absolutely complete, has been done in us without qualification and without restriction.

This was foretold even before the time of Christ. In Ezekiel 36:26,27 God said what He would do for His people:

> 'A new heart I will give you, and a new spirit I will put within you; and I will take out of your flesh the heart of stone and give you a heart of flesh. And I will put My spirit within you, and cause you to walk in My statutes and be careful to observe My ordinances'.

There is a similar promise in Jeremiah 31:33,34:

> 'This is the covenant which I will make with the house of Israel after those days, says the Lord: I will put My law within them, and I will write it upon their hearts; and I will be their God, and they shall be My people. And no longer shall each man teach his neighbour and each his brother, saying, "Know the Lord," for they shall all know Me, from the least of them to the greatest, says the Lord; for I will forgive their iniquity, and I will remember their sin no more.'

A new heart, on which, as part of its essential nature, there is written the very law of God: this is the gospel. All that God desires us to be and to do and to become is written on our new hearts, which He gives us by the Holy Spirit.

This is essential Christianity: a new heart. It is not something external, something imposed upon our personalities, but an inward life which begins from completeness. We can see from our own experience that forgiveness is not enough. People say, 'If only I had my life over again.' If we did have our lives over again and we still had the same hearts, the same personalities, we would do exactly the same things again. Forgiveness is not enough. Challenge, even, is not enough, because the truth of the matter is not only that we are *not able* to be good, we *do not want* to be good. There is a bias and a perversity in the constitution of our fallen personality. Example is not enough. Some preachers hold up Jesus Christ as the example of how men ought to live. That can be demoralising because it is beyond us.

One commentary illustrates it this way: imagine someone bringing you a copy of Shakespeare's 'King Lear' or 'Macbeth' and saying to you, 'Read these thoroughly as examples and go and write a play as good as these.' You could not do it. It is like sitting down to listen to a Brahms or Beethoven Symphony, and having someone say, 'You go and compose a symphony like that.' How could we? We have not the genius of a Shakespeare or a Brahms or a Beethoven. Granted! But if the genius of a Brahms or a Beethoven or a Shakespeare could come into our heart and life, dwelling within our life, moving throughout the whole of our personality, could we not do it? Yes. The genius, the Spirit of none other than Jesus Christ, the Holy Spirit, dwells in our hearts so that there is nothing that Jesus would have us do that is outwith the bounds of possibility for us.

The Spirit of God is mentioned right through the Bible from the very beginning (Genesis 1:2) but He came in a special way after the death, resurrection and ascension of Christ. On the evening before His crucifixion Jesus taught His disciples about the Holy

Spirit.

> 'I will pray the Father, and He will give you
> another Counsellor, to be with you for ever, even
> the Spirit of truth, whom the world cannot
> receive, because it neither sees Him nor knows
> Him; you know Him, for He dwells with you and
> *will be in you*' (John 14:16, 17).

> 'The Counsellor, the Holy Spirit, whom the
> Father will send in My name, He will teach you
> all things and bring to your remembrance all that
> I have said to you' (John 14:26).

> 'It is to your advantage that I go away, for if I do
> not go away, the Counsellor will not come to you;
> but if I go, I will send Him to you' (John 16:7).

Jesus had spoken about the Holy Spirit much earlier.
Think, for example, of His words to Nicodemus (John
3:1-15): 'That which is born of the flesh is flesh,' and can
never be anything else but 'flesh', perhaps educated,
cultured, refined, religious, but still 'flesh'. 'That which
is born of the Spirit is spirit,' something quite different.
'Do not marvel that I said to you, you must be born anew,'
born from above, born of God.

We cannot understand, nor can we fully experience
in our lives, what is means to be a Christian apart from
acquiring a grasp of the truth concerning the person and
the work of the Holy Spirit. The fundamental lesson to
grasp is that the forgiveness of sins and the gift of the
Holy Spirit go together. These two are one, and what
God has joined together we must not separate. To
receive Christ is to receive the Spirit in all His fullness.
To be a Christian is to be born of the Spirit, born into a
new life, a new dimension of experience.

> 'But to all who received Him (Christ), who
> believed in His name, He gave power to become
> children of God; who were born, not of blood

(not of natural descent) nor of the will of the flesh (not by any human effort) nor of the will of man (not by the act of any other person, be he priest or layman), but of God' (John 1:12,13).

Those who come to Christ are born of the Spirit of God. Indeed it is the work of the Holy Spirit that enables them to come, and the fact of their coming to Christ is evidence of a work of God's grace in their hearts.

A Christian is also one who is led by the Spirit. 'All who are led (on) by the Spirit of God, are sons of God' (Romans 8:14). And the Spirit of God leads us on, not as a mother with a toddler, but as the Captain of the Lord's host. There is nothing feeble or pathetic about being a Christian. It is the most virile kind of life that can be known. The whole of Romans 8, especially verses 9-13, tells us that to be a Christian is to be one who lives *in* the Holy Spirit, *by* the Holy Spirit, *with* the Holy Spirit.

Consider the words of Philip Doddridge in the Paraphrase of Hebrews 13:20,21:

'Father of peace, and God of love!
We own Thy power to save,
That power by which our Shepherd rose
Victorious o'er the grave.'

When we say 'we own' God's power to save we are not merely acknowledging it. Even the Devil acknowledges, recognises as a fact, the power of God unto salvation, but the acknowledging of that power is not the same as possessing it. As Christians we do not merely acknowledge, we have in our possession that same power by which Jesus Christ was raised from the dead. The power of the resurrection, the victory of Jesus over sin and death and hell is our possession by the Holy Spirit. By faith in the facts we must prove it to be so even to the triumphing over sins and situations which have dogged our Christian life and made it a failure for years. We must get it into our dull minds and sluggish hearts that there is no reason in the world why we should be defeated, limited, or poverty-stricken Christians. Let it be said again and again, 'Think what Spirit dwells within you.'

But directly after the resurrection the disciples had not grasped these truths, and the risen Lord promised them that after His ascension the Holy Spirit would come to them with power (Luke 24:49; Acts 1:8). Turn to the story of Pentecost (Acts 2) where we read of the clear fulfilment of that promise. What a change there was in Peter! We find him preaching to the people, 'Jesus Christ and Him crucified'.

> 'Now when they heard this they were cut to the heart, and said to Peter and the rest of the apostles, "Brethren, what shall we do?" And Peter said to them, "Repent, and be baptized every one of you in the name of Jesus Christ for the forgiveness of your sins; and you shall receive the gift of the Holy Spirit. For the promise is to you and to your children and to all that are far off, every one whom the Lord our God calls to Him." '

The forgiveness of sins and the gift of the Holy Spirit go together.

We do well to ask simply and directly, 'Do *we* believe in the Holy Spirit?' Many would answer that they are unsure and even ignorant about Him, and that could well indicate the explanation of the unsatisfactory condition of some Christians' lives, their witness and their service. There is Scripture warrant for such a suggestion in the story in Acts 19:1-8. When Paul came to the city of Ephesus, he found a group of people who called themselves Christians, which was not really surprising in view of the tremendous preaching that was going on.

Paul associated himself with the people and then began to be perplexed. He could see that they behaved in a way that was seemingly Christian. He listened to them and could see that they believed in God, that they knew about Jesus Christ, and about the facts of His life, His death and His resurrection. Their sincerity was obvious. Yet there was something wrong. Their lives and their religion seemed strangely negative, weak and joyless. There were only a dozen men there, and we may assume that the work was not growing. Where was the drive and enthusiasm the apostles expected to find among those who called themselves by the name of Jesus Christ? One could almost be describing the average church congregation on a Sunday morning! Their religion seemed to be something that was carried and organised by them rather than something that had the mastery over them. They did not seem to be like men and women who had been gripped by something greater, fuller and more glorious than themselves.

Paul gathered them round, expressed his concern, and asked, 'Did you receive the Holy Ghost when you believed?' Paul asked because he was aware that, in believing in Jesus Christ, he himself had been born anew of the Spirit of God, and the eternal Spirit of the living God dwelt in his heart and life. Paul emphasised this in all his preaching and in his letters, as Romans and Ephesians make plain. To Paul, salvation was a thing of power and enabling by the indwelling Spirit. But these 'disciples', who had believed sincerely what they had been told, had to confess that they had not been *told* about the Holy Spirit. The preaching had been defective: they had heard a limited gospel from a limited preacher.

Paul's ministry marked the turning-point in their lives. He preached more than is recorded; then as he

121

laid his hands on them (which on other occasions he did not do), these believers received the Holy Spirit and they spoke with 'tongues', seemingly in the same way as others had done on the Day of Pentecost. There is no suggestion that during Paul's three months' ministry the same pattern of laying on of hands and tongues was repeated. But now these men believed the tremendous fact that all the vital merit, victory, power and possibility of the life, death and resurrection of Jesus Christ was made effective in the life of the individual believer by the Holy Spirit coming and dwelling in his heart and life. It dawned on them that they had all this in their personal possession.

We are not to be distracted by whether or not we have had the 'experience' these Ephesians had. We are dealing with the *facts* of salvation, and facts stand independent of 'feelings'. Our concern is to believe the facts. By the regenerating power of the Holy Spirit all the virtue and victory of the death and resurrection of Jesus Christ is our personal possession, dwelling in our hearts, to be made effective in our lives from day to day. We are reborn to newness of life, not by outward constraint but by inner dynamic. People sing the words, 'Spirit of the living God, fall afresh on me,' but that form of expression is defective, because the power of God in Jesus Christ by the Holy Spirit does not come upon us by outward constraint or influence, but rather as a deep well of the water of life springing up within us, because God the Holy Spirit dwells in our hearts by faith.

The gospel has to do with the power of God unto salvation (Romans 1:16), and that power by the Holy Spirit dwells in our hearts if we are believers. It is not a portion of the Spirit we have, for the Holy Spirit is a person and cannot be divided. We are not given the Spirit in instalments, not some of the Spirit now and some later, although it takes a lifetime to discover and prove His presence and power. God the Holy Spirit, in all the completeness of His divine life and power, indwells the life of every believer.

All this truth does, of course, present a challenge, and calls us to examine our Christian lives in a day-to-day context. Are we dull and jaded, more likely to put people off Jesus than to attract them to Him? Are we more of a grumbling, discontented, carping, complaining, miserable, dispirited person than someone who is aware of the fact that all the life of God is in our heart? Do we go out to work on a Monday after Sunday worship dejected and self-centred, or do we go out with a lilt in our heart and a spring in our step, because our life is none other than the life of Christ within us? Are we the kind of Christian whose life is marked by the dynamic, the blessing, the attractiveness and the fruit of the Holy Spirit? If not, why not? Have we by unbelief and unwillingness shut up the Holy Spirit, imprisoning Him in our hearts, refusing to let Him do what is His sovereign desire: to bring every thought and every capacity of life and personality into conformity to Jesus Christ? (2 Corinthians 10:5).

It was an awareness of the fact that all the living power and possibility of God indwelt their lives by the Holy Spirit that sent out the early Christians, such as Paul, to turn the world upside down, singing as they went, singing as they suffered, singing as they died, 'I can do all things through Christ, who strengthens me' (Philippians 4:13).

In 2 Corinthians 5:17 (AV), we read, 'If any man be in Christ, he is a new creature: old things are passed away; behold, all things are become new.' If he has come in faith to Christ for forgiveness, then he has received what God promised, a new heart and a new life by the gift of the Holy Spirit. He may not feel new, and may not yet appear to his friends to be new. He may not be aware of any subjective change and may be virtually ignorant of all these things, but if he has come to Christ, this is what has happened. He is a new creature. The person he was before he came to Christ has passed away. He is a new person. It will be only a matter of time before this begins to have an effect on the whole of life.

> 'Do you not know that your body is a temple of the Holy Spirit within you, which you have from God? You are not your own ...' (1 Corinthians 6:19).

We are not our own any longer. We belong to Him who bought us at the price of His death on the cross. We as individuals (and also as the church) are the temple of the Holy Spirit; and a temple is a place where a divine person dwells, a place set apart to be 'holy unto the Lord'.

There is no doubt whatever that the Holy Spirit, having taken up His permanent residence in our hearts, will soon make changes. It is one thing to live in a house by yourself, but if someone comes to live with you, you soon become aware of their presence. Things cannot be the same as living on your own. And so it is with the Holy Spirit.

> 'And because you are sons, God has sent the Spirit of His Son into your hearts, crying "Abba! Father!" ' (Galatians 4:6).

The Spirit of Jesus Christ the Son of God, working in our hearts, creates a love for the Father like His own, which makes us want to speak to the Father. It is not surprising that we begin to want to pray. There may have been a time when praying seemed pointless, unnatural, and a burdensome duty, but it is not so now. God has put the Spirit of His own Son in our hearts, and that

Spirit is prompting us to speak to God and to call Him Father.

> 'But you are not in the flesh, you are in the Spirit, if the Spirit of God really dwells in you. Any one who does not have the Spirit of Christ does not belong to Him' (Romans 8:9).

You cannot have the Spirit of God, the Spirit of Christ, the Holy Spirit in your heart without coming to Jesus. If you have not come to Jesus you do not have the Spirit; but if you have come to Jesus then you *have* the Spirit. You cannot be a Christian without having the Holy Spirit. And, because the Spirit is a person, then He is either there 'properly' or not at all.

This is gospel truth: the facts about salvation which have to do with the power of God *for us*. In Ephesians 3:16, Paul prays for the Christians at Ephesus that:

> 'according to the riches of His glory He may grant you to be strengthened with might through His Spirit in the inner man.'

We may be tempted to say, 'If that could happen to me, I believe that even I could be a real Christian.' But this is exactly what it means to be a Christian! Look at the words. There is nothing parsimonious or miserly about God. When He does a thing, He does it gloriously. 'That He would grant you according to (on the scale of) the riches of His glory to be strengthened with might (the word is literally 'dynamic') by His Spirit in the inner man.' Paul's prayer continues:

> '... that Christ may dwell in your hearts through faith; that you, being rooted and grounded in love, may have power to comprehend with all the saints what is the breadth and length and height and depth, and to know the love of Christ which surpasses knowledge, that you may be filled with all the fullness of God' (Ephesians 3:17-19).

125

Such a glorious possibility does not speak of a time when we are 'far on' in Christian life, aged saints of God. All the fullness of God is in Christ, and when we come to Christ, Christ comes to us, to dwell in our hearts, so that at our conversion we are filled with all the fullness of God. Little wonder Paul breaks into a doxology of praise:

> 'Now unto Him that is able to do exceeding abundantly above all that we ask or think, according to the power that worketh in us' (by the Holy Spirit) 'unto Him be glory in the church by Christ Jesus throughout all ages, world without end' (Ephesians 3:20, 21 AV).

This is a subject to rejoice in. All the riches of the grace, the glory and the power of God dwell in the heart of the believer by the Holy Spirit. That Holy Spirit is given when we first come to Christ. It is almost certainly true of all of us that we have not realised or appropriated or experienced His presence and power as we could and should have done, for personal holiness and for Christian service. We need the reminder, 'Think what Spirit dwells within you.'

> 'For in Him the whole fullness of deity dwells bodily, and you have come to fullness of life in Him,' (that is, you are filled full with all the fullness of God in Him) ... (Colossians 2:9,10).

This is what we mean when we say, 'I believe in the Holy Spirit.' He is the third person of the Eternal Trinity, who brings all the benefit and power of the salvation that was accomplished in the death and resurrection of Jesus Christ to us, to be within us, our present possession.

CHAPTER ELEVEN

THE HOLY SPIRIT (2)

The subject of the Holy Spirit has tended to be one which bristles with difficulties, beset by misunderstandings and imbalance. In this second study, our aim is to seek a greater practical understanding of the place and the power of the Holy Spirit in our daily lives, and at the same time to keep as far from controversy as possible.

In recent days there has emerged a new emphasis on the person and the work of the Holy Spirit. There has in fact been a stirring of God the Holy Spirit on many different levels in the life of the Christian church, for which we can do nothing other than give thanks to God. Yet at the same time, we are solemnly put under obligation by the Scriptures to 'test the spirits' (1 John 4:1). We are not to accept everything that is 'spirit' as being necessarily of the good Spirit of God. We must examine the spirits, their work, their influence, and all that they seem to produce in the life of the Christian church. Only that which is biblical, that which is beneficial to the whole church in terms of moral character and spiritual service is of God.

In the New Testament we learn that in the city of Corinth the fellowship of the church of Jesus Christ was divided, and distracted from service, because of the competitive jealousies between the 'haves' and the 'have nots', especially with regard to one or two specific gifts of the Holy Spirit. The more obvious, unusual and ecstatic gifts were the focus of attention and the other more ordinary gifts of the Spirit largely ignored.

Now, if a spirit emerges in a fellowship that disturbs and destroys its peace and unity while countenancing gross moral misbehaviour, as in Corinth (1 Corinthians 5:1,2), so that the public testimony of the congregation is dishonoured, can that spirit be the good Spirit of God?

There is a fundamental principle at stake. We must always test our experiences by the Word of God; we must not interpret the Word of God by our experiences. Our experiences are subjective; they may be right, they may be wrong. The Word of God is objective; it stands clear and categorical. Every experience then must be taken and examined in the light of the Word of God. This is tremendously important with regard to the work of the Holy Spirit, in terms of our moral sanctification, and our daily practice as professing Christians in a world that still rejects Jesus Christ, the Son of God.

Whenever we find any extraordinary manifestations that claim to be of the Holy Spirit we should initially reserve our judgment, because, as Jesus said to Nicodemus, the Spirit of God is like the wind; He is free to work as He chooses. There is no rigid pattern or absolute conformity with regard to the Spirit's working to be found in the whole of Scripture. But wherever God's Spirit is at work the effect will be to glorify Christ, to take the person of Christ and set Him pre-eminently in the foreground of everything, and cause everything to be in subjection to Him. Wherever the Holy Spirit is at work, He will point not to Himself but to Christ and to the facts of the gospel. Jesus made this clear in John 15:26 and 16:13,14: 'He will glorify Me.' Similarly on the Day of Pentecost the preaching was about Christ, which some of the advocates of the new Pentecostalism forget. Peter declared,

> "... God has made Him both Lord and Christ, this Jesus whom you crucified."

Now when they heard this they were cut to the heart, and said to Peter and the rest of the apostles, "Brethren, what shall we do?" And Peter said to them, "Repent, and be baptised every one of you in the name of Jesus Christ for the forgiveness of your sins; and you shall receive the gift of the Holy Spirit. For the promise is to you and to your children and to all that are far off, every one whom the Lord our God calls to Him" ' (Acts 2:36-39).

They were not baptised in the name of the Holy Spirit, but in the name of Jesus Christ. They heard the word that testified of Christ; by the power of the Holy Spirit they were brought to Christ for the forgiveness of sins, and they received the gift of the Holy Spirit.

'And they devoted themselves to the apostles' teaching and fellowship, to the breaking of bread and the prayers' (Acts 2:42).

The doctrine concerned Christ and Him crucified. The preaching concerned the cross, the finished work of salvation: a once-for-all perfect victory over sins, sin and Satan. The message of the gospel is that this glorious salvation, in all its threefold dimension, is given to men when they come to Christ.

Do not become preoccupied and distracted by the supernatural signs on the Day of Pentecost. In Acts 2:1-4 a group of some one hundred and twenty disciples received the gift of the Holy Spirit, attended by miraculous manifestations, but in 2:41-47 a great company of some three thousand received the same forgiveness and the same gift of the Holy Spirit without anything untoward or outward happening. We may not insist that the Holy Spirit's presence, power and activity are always attended by certain evidences.

In one sense the doctrine of the Holy Spirit is a mystery. As Jesus said to Nicodemus, 'The wind, the Spirit, blows where it will, you hear the sound (you see the working of the power) but you cannot explain it.' The Spirit is like the wind, a sweet breath that blows away the murky mists and fogs of sin. But wind can be harnessed. You may not understand the wind, but if you are at sea and you hoist a sail, instantly, as the wind breathes, the power begins to move your vessel along. The Holy Spirit is further spoken of as oil that anoints, comforts and is fuel for light and fire; as fire itself that warms and purges; as water that washes and revives; and as a dove that speaks of peace. Scripture speaks of the Holy Spirit as the Spirit of holiness, the Spirit of truth, of wisdom, of love, power and, indeed, of a sound mind (2 Timothy 1:7); the Spirit of sonship that makes us call God our Father (Romans 8:14,15). The Holy Spirit is also the Spirit of prayer and supplication. He is that Spirit by whose presence in our hearts and by whose all-sufficient ministry every need and every aspect of experience is met, not from without, but from within.

While it is, of course, both difficult and dangerous to try to systematise the work of the Holy Spirit, we can think of it in three aspects: *for* us, *in* us, and *through* us. We could use slightly more technical terms and speak of the work of the Holy Spirit in respect of salvation, sanctification, and service. There is in fact no limit to what God can do with us and for us by the indwelling Holy Spirit.

The work of the Holy Spirit *for us* in respect of salvation is, to use the technical term, the work of regeneration, causing us to be re-born, to be brought to life from a condition of spiritual death. It is expressed clearly in Ephesians 2:1,2:

> 'You He made alive, when you were dead through the trespasses and sins in which you once walked, following the course of this world, following the prince of the power of the air, the

spirit that is now at work in the sons of disobedience.'

We may not have felt we were dead in sin. Such a thought may never have crossed our minds. But this is the truth, and apart from the saving power of God we are and we remain spiritually dead. Nor were we free agents before we were converted. We were slaves of sin, whether we knew it or not.

'Among these we all once lived in the passions of our flesh, following the desires of body and mind, and so we were by nature children of wrath, like the rest of mankind. But God, who is rich in mercy, out of the great love with which He loved us, even when we were dead through our trespasses, made us alive together with Christ (by grace you have been saved), and raised us up with Him, and made us sit with Him in the heavenly places in Christ Jesus' (Ephesians 2:3-6).

God came to us in Jesus Christ by the Holy Spirit when we were spiritually dead and helpless in trespasses and sins, and, by the power of His Holy Spirit, we were made alive from the dead.

It is a miracle of sovereign grace. Understand it in terms of the story of creation in the Book of Genesis, where we have a picture of chaos, disorder, and darkness. Then the Spirit of God brooded upon the face of the deep; God spoke His word, and out of the darkness and disorder there came life, order, peace and power. So it is with us. God, by His Holy Spirit, regenerates us, quickens us, brings us to life, and behold, we are alive spiritually. To begin with we may not be aware of what is happening. Still, we begin to hear the gospel with a new understanding, a new hunger, and a new interest; then we begin to respond to the preaching of the name of Jesus Christ; and in due time, in conscious choice, we come to Christ, and that is our conversion. It all began with the miracle of the 'quickening' of the Holy Spirit.

No one can really explain the miracle of life, but we do know when a new life is born. In a maternity hospital, what they look for in the very instant of birth is a cry to signify that life is there. So it is in the things of the Spirit. A new-born life stirs within us, and there begin to come into evidence new desires, new hopes and new appetites. But this is only the beginning.

Having been born of the Spirit of God, and raised to newness of life, the possibilities of holiness are now within our grasp, and our consideration moves on from the thought of salvation to that of sanctification. This is the work of the Spirit *in us*. He takes the salvation that is now there within us and constrains us to realise it in its power and blessing in daily experience. It is a tragedy when something is there in our possession and we do not use it. We read in the press about some pathetic beggar who has lived in rags, scrounging a crust of bread to eat, huddling in a corner to keep warm. Then after he is dead, it is discovered that he left thousands of pounds. There was no need for him to live such a miserable, beggarly existence. He had riches he never used and life could have been so different. Think of our resources as believers for, in Christ, we are spiritual millionaires. Are we not prepared to make use of our possessions?

The work of the Spirit of God within us is to teach, encourage and enable us to take all the treasure that is at our disposal and use it. This leads us into conflict, because the new life by the Spirit of God within us does not automatically set aside the old.

'The desires of the flesh are against the Spirit,
and the desires of the Spirit are against the flesh;

for these are opposed to each other ...'
(Galatians 5:17).

What an unhappy home there is within us sometimes,
what conflict and fighting, as the Spirit of God asserts
the crown rights of the Redeemer Jesus Christ! The
Spirit says, 'This is the life we shall live', but the carnal
dregs of the flesh within us, trying to pull us down, say,
'Let's have a bit more of that other life. Let's go back
like the pig to the mire.' The Spirit of God asserts the
claims of Christ and pleads the cause of Christ saying,
'No, this is the way. Enter in and possess your
possessions.'

The Authorised Version expresses the truth vividly
saying that 'the Spirit lusts against the flesh and the flesh
against the Spirit.' But it is not a battle of equals. There
is no need at any time, not even once, for the flesh to win,
because Christ by the Holy Spirit is within us. His victory
over the world, the flesh and the Devil is ours, though the
Bible never says that we can be *sinless*. If we say we have
no sin we deceive ourselves (1 John 1:8); but the Bible
most certainly does say that we can be victorious. Turn
to Luke 4:1,2,13 and compare the experience of our Lord
Jesus Christ:

> 'And Jesus, full of the Holy Spirit, returned from
> the Jordan, and was led by the Spirit for forty
> days in the wilderness, tempted by the devil.
> And when the devil had ended every temptation,
> he departed from Him until an opportune time.'

Think of these verses in terms of the doctrine of the
fullness of the Holy Spirit. To be filled with the Spirit of
God does not ensure immunity from temptation, but
rather exposure to it. The temptations are not
necessarily confined to the realm of the lusts of the flesh,
but rather, as in the story of the temptation of Jesus in
the wilderness, they can be temptations on the highest,

133

most all-embracing, most spiritual level that any mortal can ever know. Think of the different temptations of Jesus: Make these stones bread; Cast yourself from the temple; All these kingdoms will I give you. In each temptation the essential choice before Jesus was the way of self or the way of God. In each wave of temptation, the Spirit of God revealed the Satanic device and gave Jesus victory. It is when we are filled with the Spirit of God and walking in the Spirit of God that we are led by that same Spirit into the fuller and deeper realm of all that God has prepared for us. It is bound to be a greater conflict than it was before we were converted.

There are Christians who do foolish things in an attempt to be spiritual. They abuse their bodies and their personalities, they neglect every human provision of God, claiming that God the Holy Spirit will look after them. It is an extravagance which draws attention to self, not to Jesus. There are people who, in the name of the Holy Spirit's work of sanctification, ignore accepted forms of dress. They are not going to be 'conformed' to the fashion of the world, and so they wear clothes that mark them out as different. They are sad advertisements for Jesus, because the people who see them think of them, not of Jesus. That which purports to be sanctification and humility is in fact a subtle form of pride, drawing attention to self. But the work of the Holy Spirit points away from self to Jesus.

The same kind of thing faces every preacher, because the temptation is to be so clever, so gifted and attractive in his preaching that people will go away from church saying, 'Wasn't he great?' Which he? The preacher or Jesus? If people go away thinking the preacher was great then the preacher has failed. All his eloquence, his passion, his facility with the Scripture count for nothing because he has drawn attention to himself. The Holy

Spirit would point to Jesus.

The Spirit of God within us does constant battle with this powerful carnal self. Martin Luther said that he was more afraid 'of the great Pope Self' within his members than all the other Popes of Christendom. At a convention where there were two speakers, one preached on the story of Abraham and Isaac on Mount Moriah when Abraham was called to sacrifice Isaac. Quite legitimately he said, 'Here is the call of God for consecration. Are you prepared to sacrifice your Isaac, your dearest possession on earth?' The second preacher said, 'It is not your Isaac that God wants you to give up. It is yourself.' Self must go.

Turn to Romans 8:11-13, a very practical message:

'If the Spirit of Him who raised Jesus from the dead dwells in you, He who raised Christ Jesus from the dead will give life to your mortal bodies also through His Spirit which dwells in you. So then, brethren, we are debtors (under obligation) not to the flesh, (for it cannot give you anything) to live according to the flesh - for if you live according to the flesh you will die, but if by the Spirit you put to death the deeds of the body you will live.'

This concept of putting to death is a very strong one. It speaks of an attitude of ruthless rejection of and resistance towards everything that is contrary to Christ.

Right through the sixth chapter of Paul's Letter to the Romans there is an emphasis on the choice that has to be made on the basis of the fact that, in the death and resurrection of Jesus Christ, sin has been dethroned. Sin as a power is in the condemned cell. It may batter on the door of the cell but, unless we turn traitor to Christ and ourselves and open the door, sin cannot harm us. We have the gospel promise, 'Sin shall not have dominion over you!' (Romans 6:14 AV). The Holy Spirit within us says, 'And I will see to it.' That is the work of the Spirit within us.

As we reckon on the fact that the victory of Jesus Christ is our possession by the Holy Spirit within us, and as we walk in the Spirit, led along by the Spirit, all the desire of God is fulfilled, and in every facet of our personality we are fashioned in holiness. It is not cold, pious holiness, which is so unattractive, but the holiness we see in Jesus Christ: holiness that is natural, gracious, and human. Indeed, it is holiness that has a sense of humour, which a Christian can afford to have for the simple reason that nothing is in doubt any more.

Finally, there is the work of the Spirit *through* us. We cannot imagine Jesus being selfish. Nor can we think of anyone who is born of the Spirit of God wanting to keep all the mighty treasure of the gospel to himself. Jesus said:

> 'You shall receive power when the Holy Spirit has come upon you; and you shall be My witnesses in Jerusalem and in all Judea and Samaria and to the end of the earth' (Acts 1:8).

Whatever form of Christian service God calls us to, no Christian is allowed to say 'I am not able', because it is not true. By the Holy Spirit who dwells in our hearts we are enabled to be witnesses.

But if Christians *are* filled with the Spirit, and thereby all the potential of the victory of Christ is within their grasp, why are so many Christians often dull, defeated, unattractive people? Breaking into the great sermon of Stephen the first martyr, we read:

> 'You stiff-necked people, uncircumcised in heart and ears, you always resist the Holy Spirit. As your fathers did, so do you' (Acts 7:51).

This is why many Christians are living lives that are

unsatisfactory in terms of moral victory and spiritual fruitfulness. They are resisting the Holy Spirit.

God the Holy Spirit speaks to us concerning our inheritance in Christ, urging us to go on with Christ, but we so often retreat into the privacy of our own thoughts and say, 'No thank you, God.' I wonder if some who read these pages should be on the mission field or in the ministry, and should have been years ago. I wonder if some should be active in personal witness and in commitment to the work of their own church, but it is not so. Why? Have you been resisting the Holy Spirit?

We may not be resisting the Holy Spirit in terms of willingness to serve, but it is possible to grieve the Holy Spirit in other ways:

> 'Do not grieve the Holy Spirit of God, in whom you were sealed for the day of redemption. Let all bitterness and wrath and anger and clamour and slander be put away from you, with all malice, and be kind to one another, tenderhearted, forgiving one another, as God in Christ forgave you' (Ephesians 4:30-32).

If we are not prepared to be like that, we grieve, that is, we cause sorrow to, the Holy Spirit by the selfishness of our hearts which blights the unity of the fellowship.

Scripture speaks also by way of warning:

> 'Do not quench the Spirit' (1 Thessalonians 5:19).

The word 'quench' is a word that speaks of damping down a fire. We tend not to be aware of the great desire of God the Holy Spirit within our hearts to make us disciples and witnesses to Jesus Christ.

What then is the Spirit of God trying to produce through us? We can sum it up very simply: fellowship and fruit; fellowship unto service, and fruit in Christian character. The Spirit of God seeks to bring us together because it is only in the fellowship of Christ that we are able to grow and to become all that God desires us to become. You cannot be a 'loner' in the things of the Spirit. That is why we read so much in Corinthians about the 'body' of believers. Members need each other because they are part of a true working body. Look at 1 Corinthians 12:12 ff. and compare this with Ephesians 4:1-6.

To see the fruit of the Spirit turn to Galatians 5:22-23. We have nine statements concerning it: the first three inward, the second three manward, the third three Godward. The fruit of the Spirit is love. What a human word it is! And a 'sanctification' by the indwelling Spirit that does not make us human like Jesus is a fraud. Love, joy, peace, are beautiful words, so are long-suffering, gentleness, goodness, faith, meekness and self-control. Against such there is no law. The ultimate work of the Holy Spirit is to make us think of the person of Jesus Christ. He brings us to Christ, to root us in Christ, to make us a fellowship in Christ, to mature us in Christ, to give us the victory in Christ, to build us up in Christ, and to make us like Christ.

That is the work of the Spirit. That is the sanctification of the Spirit. That is the fruit of the Spirit. Ordinary people like us in our daily lives, knowing all the conflicts fundamental to spiritual life, begin to show in our human personalities the graces of Jesus Christ. The Holy Spirit in our hearts works to that end. Don't resist Him. Don't grieve Him. Don't quench Him. Let Him do His blessed work and bring us in the wholeness of our redeemed personalities to the very feet of the Son of God. This is the fullness of the Spirit.

Some may ask about the 'gifts of the Spirit' and we must be clear that no-one should insist that certain gifts are basic, necessary and always given. There is nothing to suggest that 'gifted' people (humanly or spiritually) are better or more necessary than others. It is God who gives or withholds, and He does so in His perfect wisdom for the blessing of His people and the furtherance of His work. In that work, God is pleased to choose the weak things of the world so that no mere man or woman will glory or boast in His sight.

Finally, remember Jesus' words in John 7:37-39 when on the last great day of the feast He said:

> 'If any one thirst, let him come to Me and drink. He who believes in Me, as the scripture has said, "Out of his heart shall flow rivers of living water." Now this He said about the Spirit, which those who believed in Him were to receive.'

Out of that person's inner being, by the Holy Spirit, there shall flow rivers of living water. Archbishop William Temple once said, 'No one can possess or be indwelt by the Holy Spirit of God and keep that Spirit to himself.' If He is there, He will flow forth. If there is no flowing forth, it is because the Spirit of God is not there. Here is the picture. We keep coming to Christ to drink the water of life, and, as we keep on coming, by the miracle of God's grace, as the sanctifying work of the Spirit proceeds, we become fountains of life-giving water that reaches other people.

I once complained about the cost of the ministry to my brother, a minister in Edinburgh, saying, 'It is a case of giving, giving, all the time.' He replied, 'If you keep at the Fountainhead you will never run dry.' There is no reason why any Christian should ever run dry. We believe in the Holy Spirit, and because of that Spirit's dwelling in our hearts we are spiritual millionaires with resources beyond measurement.

CHAPTER TWELVE

THE HOLY CATHOLIC CHURCH

In the contemporary religious scene there are two serious and significant defects. There is a devaluation of doctrine, as if sound doctrine were no longer necessary so long as Christian experience is 'good' or 'thrilling', and there is a devaluation of the church, as if its life, fellowship and work were no longer necessary for the furtherance of God's work in the world. But all through Scripture we see believers gathered, organised and identified as the people of God in an alien world.

There are many who are all too willing to pronounce with authority, and to tell you everything you need to know about God, about the church and about any other religious subject you care to mention! Many of these opinionated people never read their Bible and seldom, if ever, go to church, except for such occasions as weddings and baptisms, and even then for sentimental and social reasons rather than theological or spiritual ones. All this does not deter them however, for they are their own ultimate authority in all things and are content to be so.

Such people declare, with a great show of wisdom, that you can be a perfectly good Christian without going to church. That is simply not true! People affirm that you can worship God just as well, perhaps even better, walking on the hills as you can cooped up in a building going through the dull routine of a church service. The truth about such people is that they are not really dealing with God at all. They may have some stirring of their mental and emotional processes, but that is not the same as worship. They may have some awareness of 'divinity' but that is not a recognition of the God of Christian revelation. Something far more specific is needed before faith begins, and then faith needs to be nurtured and instructed. This is where the importance of the church begins to be seen.

Confusion arises because people have not grasped what the church is and what it is for. It is not a building, humble or grand, although buildings are useful things. It is not a social club, although people try hard to make it so, to provide cheap accommodation for a variety of secular pursuits, physical or cultural, sometimes made 'religious' by attaching an epilogue at the end of the evening's proceedings. The church is not a meeting-place for middle-class people with inclinations towards religion (provided it is not taken too far), nor is it a secluded shelter for ultra-holy people whose Christianity is not virile enough to stand up to the rigours of life in a real world. Some think of the church as an organisation which makes the minimum demand on its associates and members, keeping the door so widely open that anyone so inclined can belong, with or without faith, believing or not believing even in God Himself. Such a 'church' is nothing at all. It will have no impact on anyone, and will be continuingly irrelevant to man's experience. Others try to make the church the ultimate 'closed shop', so impeccably and implacably guarded against any possible departure from absolute orthodoxy in every part that it becomes the ultimate in pharisaic legalism and hypocrisy, wherein the really important thing is outward conformity regardless of the state of the heart.

It is vital in the understanding of the church to recognise at the outset that it is not a human organisation at all. Demolish all the church buildings, disband all associated organisations, stop all activity of every kind and churches as we know them would disappear (and lots of members would never notice), but still the church would remain. So long as you have two or three believers you have the church in the world, the holy, catholic or universal, apostolic church, because it is God's creation and not man's. Jesus said:

'... I will build My church, and the gates of hell shall not prevail against it' (Matthew 16:18 AV).

It is not man's church. It is Christ's church. He alone brought it into being and maintains its life and existence. Always remember that in these words of Jesus just quoted, the picture is not of the church on the defensive, standing firm against the assaults of hell, although that is a glorious picture and true. The real picture is of the gates of hell reeling back in confusion and defeat in the face of the irresistible *advance* of the holy, catholic, apostolic church of Jesus Christ. Some people are confused by the word 'catholic', thinking it means the same as Roman Catholic, but there is no thought of this in the Creed. It is merely an old word meaning the same as 'universal'.

The church is holy because it is the work of God in Jesus Christ, and is a unique spiritual creation. It is catholic or universal because it is not confined by any artificial man-made barriers, nor can it ever be the possession of any group or class. It is apostolic because it is grounded in and governed by the doctrine of the apostles. The church is God's creation, not man's. It begins in the sovereign activity of God, and it consists of all those in every age of history who have responded in faith to the glorious initiative and invitation of God, who has worked salvation and life in the death and resurrection of His Son Jesus Christ our Lord. In answering the call of God's grace we are brought into salvation and into fellowship, to be a people for God's own possession (1 Peter 2:9), to show forth His praises.

To understand the church we must first grasp what it means to be a Christian. A Christian is one who is Christ's, that is, he belongs to Christ; he is not his own, but is totally, utterly and exclusively belonging to another. A Christian is one who has been brought into Christ, one who has Christ brought into him, into his heart and life; one who, by Christ, has been brought into the kingdom of God's salvation. A Christian is one who, in Christ, has as his present possession the forgiveness of sins and, with this, the gift of the Holy Spirit in the entirety of His person and power. By that Holy Spirit dwelling in his heart the Christian is seen to be a man who has been born again, raised from the dead to newness of life, life that is eternal in its nature, dimension and fullness. A Christian is a new creation: he has been lifted out of the kingdom of darkness into the kingdom of the Son of God's love (Colossians 1:13). It is something tremendous and dynamic to be a Christian. It is life that is abundant, and it is eternally sure because it is the work of God through Jesus Christ by His Holy Spirit.

The Bible is quite clear that religion must be personal or it is nothing. There must be a personal response to God's initiative of grace, but that experience of God's grace never remains individualistic or isolated. No Christian ever 'goes it alone' because if the same Holy Spirit indwells every single believer then we are inevitably and vitally one, and we belong together. Because we are all one in Christ by that Holy Spirit, we are drawn together and come together, and in that coming there is constituted and made manifest the church of Jesus Christ. We come together and gather in church not in order to make us Christians, but because we *are* Christians, and in that fellowship of faith and life we grow in Christ to full stature of character, worship and service. This is the holy, catholic, apostolic church and we begin to see it as anything but dull, and certainly far from being irrelevant in the affairs of men.

Consider certain passages of Scripture which together build up a picture and give an exposition of the church. There are many such passages, and we are necessarily selective.

In Acts 20:28, Paul's address to the elders of the church at Ephesus, we read:

> 'Take heed to yourselves and to all the flock, in which the Holy Spirit has made you guardians, to feed the church of the Lord which He obtained with His own blood.'

We have here a picture of a Shepherd, a flock and a fold, and a tremendous purchase price of redemption that was paid to make this flock God's own possession. It is God's flock, and from the lips of His Son we learn the value of one single member of that flock. In Luke 15:1-7 we have the story of the ninety-nine sheep and the one solitary sheep that was lost. In John 10:1-16, we have the story of Jesus the Good Shepherd. The Shepherd's heart could not be content with even one sheep missing, and no effort or sacrifice was considered too much in order to recover that lost one.

In 1 Corinthians 1:2, we have the description given by Paul of the church at Corinth and again the emphasis is on the proprietary rights of God Himself:

> 'To the church of God which is at Corinth, to those sanctified in Christ Jesus, called to be saints together with all those who in every place call on the name of our Lord Jesus Christ, both their Lord and ours.'

What a glorious description this is! In a thoroughly pagan city there is found a church, a congregation of men and women who by the preaching of the gospel have been brought to faith. In the sovereign purpose of God they are set apart (sanctified) as being holy unto the Lord, called to be saints, that is, to be God's men and women, having fellowship with all those in Corinth, and in every other place world-wide, who have believed on the Lord Jesus Christ.

In 1 Peter 2:5 we read:

> 'And like living stones be yourselves built into a spiritual house, to be a holy priesthood, to offer spiritual sacrifices acceptable to God through Jesus Christ.'

Essentially we are dealing here with polished stones rather than rough-hewn ones, being built together on the foundation that is Christ to make a house for spiritual worship. Later (1 Peter 2:9), Peter speaks of our being a chosen people, a people for God's own possession, not for the enjoyment of privilege but:

> 'You are a chosen race, a royal priesthood, a holy nation, God's own people, that you may declare the wonderful deeds of Him who called you out of darkness into His marvellous light.'

Perhaps the most comprehensive statement, for our purpose, regarding the church, is found in Ephesians:

> 'But God, who is rich in mercy, out of the great love with which He loved us, even when we were dead through our trespasses, made us alive together with Christ (by grace you have been saved), and raised us up with Him, and made us sit with Him in the heavenly places in Christ Jesus, that in the coming ages He might show the immeasurable riches of His grace in kindness toward us in Christ Jesus' (2:4-7).

> 'For through Him we both have access in one Spirit to the Father. So then you are no longer strangers and sojourners, but you are fellow

citizens with the saints and members of the household of God, built upon the foundation of the apostles and prophets, Christ Jesus Himself being the cornerstone, in whom the whole structure is joined together and grows into a holy temple in the Lord; in whom you also are built into it for a dwelling place of God in the Spirit' (2:18-22).

There is almost too much truth in this passage for us to be able to grasp it. We take only the salient points in order to elucidate the nature of the church. Paul calls on the Ephesians to remember that when they were dead in trespasses and sins they were raised from the dead and made alive in Christ. It is not only *through* Christ but *in* Christ, that is, united to Christ in His death and resurrection, that we are made alive. This is salvation, and by it we are *in Christ*, made one and made members one of the other in indissoluble union. We are part of each other, sharing one life, one service, one destiny; and the sense of glorious purpose in all this simply cannot be evaded.

There is something very important here in the thought of the unifying effect of salvation. In Ephesians 2:12, there is a picture of what it means to be without God in the world: Christless, godless and hopeless.

'Remember that you were at that time separated from Christ, alienated from the commonwealth of Israel, and strangers to the covenants of promise, having no hope, and without God in the world.'

This futility, nihilism and emptiness is expressed in our generation in the disintegration of society in which men have no longer any sense of belonging or any sense of destiny. When this happens we end up in a disastrous and destructive individualism which constantly frustrates and prevents the togetherness which men and women need and crave for, as is evident from the longing words of some contemporary song lyrics. 'Lost' is indeed the word to describe this generation, and the glory of the gospel is that in Jesus Christ, and in no other way, the dissipating and divisive bias of human nature and experience is countered. Christ integrates us first within ourselves, putting our shattered personalities together again, and then He unifies us by leading the redeemed individual into fellowship with others, within which fellowship the work of grace continues and is encouraged to go on to its full fruitfulness.

The church is seen to be many made one in Christ. The Bible does not think in terms of freelance Christians who could well be called 'amputated saints', severed from the body, detached members belonging nowhere, and in consequence having neither the capacity to grow nor the opportunity to serve. In Ephesians it becomes clear that only by being what God has made us, namely part of one united whole which is the living organism or body which is the church, only then can we become all that God intends us to become and only then are we able to receive all that God desires to give (4:13-16).

Without doubt the emphasis is on many made one in inter-dependence. It is all of God's grace; consequently there is no room for inferiority or superiority complexes. All are one, big stones being needed as well as little stones to complete the building, just as cooking pots as well as best dinner-plates are essential for a successful banquet. We are together and we are one in Christ. This is the church.

Note the terms that are used in the passage from the Ephesian letter. We are no longer strangers, lodgers, passing through, having only temporary status and being allowed to remain only on sufferance. We belong! We are not outsiders! We are fellow citizens with the saints of past history who are now gathered in glory (not second-class citizens because of some past folly or inheritance or circumstance or lack). We have full rights, privileges *and* responsibilities. We are members of the household of God (an amazing description of the church), with the newborn being as much part of the family as the aged grandparents. We are children at home with the Father, a picture of unity which does not deny identity. Within the household there is a marvellous variety of individual personality and it is this which makes the life of the church so rich and fascinating. It is never a good thing when too many of one kind of people are found in a fellowship of Christ's church. If all are of the same kind, all intellectual, or professional, or artisans, then a dullness is inevitable. People of all kinds and of all ages are needed. Within this household of God (Ephesians 2:19) you are loved enough to be allowed to be yourself. Indeed you are encouraged and helped to be yourself, though this needs rules and discipline as well as freedom. You belong and you know it, and you count on it. All the thoughts of privilege, responsibility and loyalty are there, and you are not ashamed of your family.

The Ephesian passage goes on to speak of the church as a building, not of stone and lime but made of people referred to as being living stones built in, grounded in and held together by the chief cornerstone which is Christ. In union with Christ the whole building is being framed into a holy sanctuary, a permanent abode for God to dwell in by His Spirit. It is increasing in solidity, beauty and effectiveness in proportion as each stone is fashioned, polished and takes its place, so that the individual and the fellowship are both seen to be growing in grace. The objective is to provide a place for God to dwell in fellowship with His people, a place and a means by which God can manifest His glory, a place or an instrument through which He can exercise to the full His perfect power and purpose. This is the church.

Of course, when scaffolding is round a building in the process of its erection, the glory of that building is seen only in promise. When at last the scaffolding of present experience is dismantled then the glory of the church will be seen. It does not yet appear what we shall be, but in the end there will be the full shining of God's glory in the church. This final glory does not have its emphasis on the individualism of the stones, although that is preserved to the full, but on the completed church. Think of the reference in Malachi 3:17 A.V. to the making up of God's jewels. They are all precious stones and glorious in themselves, but when they are set together by a master-hand the result is a fuller glory. It is like a beautifully planned mosaic in which the parts come into their own identity and beauty *only* when they become part of the whole. This is the church, a fellowship of life in salvation in which individuality and unity are both glorious, and God comes down to stay, just as the Shekinah glory settled on the Tabernacle (Exodus 40:34).

Were this an exposition of Ephesians rather than a study on the nature of the church, we could go on at this point to elaborate on how God, by the church, both now and in the world to come, shows forth the glory of His grace to men and to devils (2:7; 3:9-11,21). He does this firstly by the individual Christian, saved in the salvation of God in Jesus Christ. But God Himself bears testimony to, and demonstrates, the wonder of His grace even more in the life of the church that is constituted by the bringing together of these individuals.

A further passage for reference is in Paul's letter to

the Romans 12:4-5, and this needs to be linked with 1 Corinthians 12:12-27, words of immense comfort and encouragement to those who tend to feel that they are too insignificant and untalented to be of much use in the fellowship and the work of the church of Jesus Christ. The point we make from Romans (and we must not forget the doctrine of salvation by grace in the early chapters of that epistle) is that the church is the body of Christ, the instrument by which He carries out and carries forward to completeness His redemptive work in the world.

The nature, life and function of the church are seen in the variety of illustrations used in Scripture. All are necessary, and we can only mention them in passing. The church is spoken of in terms of a king and his people; a master and his disciples; a shepherd and his flock; a vine and its branches; a building and the stones which comprise it; a body and its members; and perhaps most wonderfully of all, a bridegroom and his chosen bride, on whom he looks with the uniqueness of love and loyalty. Think of the wonder of the passage in Ephesians 5:25-27:

> 'Husbands, love your wives, as Christ loved the church and gave Himself up for her, that He might sanctify her, having cleansed her by the washing of water with the word, that He might present the church to Himself in splendour, without spot or wrinkle or any such thing, that she might be holy and without blemish.'

Consider also the magnificence of the ultimate glory of the church expressed in the words of Revelation 21:2-5:

> 'And I saw the holy city, new Jerusalem, coming down out of heaven from God, prepared as a bride adorned for her husband; and I heard a

great voice from the throne saying, "Behold, the dwelling of God is with men. He will dwell with them, and they shall be His people, and God Himself will be with them; He will wipe away every tear from their eyes, and death shall be no more, neither shall there be mourning nor crying nor pain any more, for the former things have passed away."

'And He who sat upon the throne said, "Behold, I make all things new." Also He said, "Write this, for these words are trustworthy and true." '

Then, over against this portrayal of the church, set one of the saddest pictures in all the Bible, that of Christ standing outside the door of the church knocking and asking for admission and scarcely being heard, except by a few:

> 'Behold, I stand at the door and knock; if any one hears My voice and opens the door, I will come in to him, and eat with him, and he with Me' (Revelation 3:20).

This is no fiction! Christ is squeezed out of the church and kept out, when the world has been allowed to invade the church. The spirit of the world is the spirit of anti-christ (1 John 5:19) and we must never forget this. If the spirit of the world is allowed to infiltrate the church, compromise its testimony, and corrupt its life, then the church becomes like salt that has lost its savour and is good for nothing. Never forget the anger of Jesus when He cleansed the temple of all that had prostituted the Father's house of prayer. The church must be the church, and if it fails or refuses so to be, it comes under the rebuke and the judgment of Christ the Lord of the church.

We do not propose to go into the realm of technical linguistics to consider the meaning of the word 'church'.

In the Greek translation of the Old Testament (Septuagint) the word 'ecclesia' (church) is used to translate two words signifying a people called by authority and assembled by appointment, there being a specific purpose in view. How truly that description fits the calling and nature and destiny of the people of Israel in the Old Testament! In the New Testament the word 'ecclesia' signifies an assembly or congregation of people called out and called together to be a significant people, again with a purpose in view. This whole concept could be grasped clearly in New Testament times, because every Greek city had its own 'ecclesia', a group of citizens appointed to represent that city and have its affairs in their safe keeping. The church is God's 'ecclesia' in the world: God's people with God's business in their hands. What a glorious, if rather frightening, calling!

Take three words from Paul's description of his apostleship in Romans 1:1 to summarise briefly the description of the church, the called and gathered people of God. They are *called*, *separated*, and *sent out*.

The church is *called* in the sense of being called out from the world of unbelief into the world of faith, and in consequence called together into an identifiable, recognisable entity. The church is different from the world, different in nature and destiny, and the two must never be confused. The world as we know it will in the fullness of time pass away, but the church of Jesus Christ will remain. She is lifted up into the purposes of God. The calling of God is effectual, and Christ will build His church and the gates of hell shall not prevail against it.

The church is also *separated* from the world, and she must recognise this to be so if there is to be an effective witness in the world. This separation is not in man-made exclusivism, which leads to the picture we have in the

Gospels of the Jewish priests gathering the skirts of their garments to themselves lest they might possibly incur defilement from contact with the world. None of that unholy and inhuman separation is seen in Jesus, who was the Friend of sinners and went to the homes of sinners (Matthew 11:19, Luke 19:5). But Scripture still describes Him as holy, harmless, undefiled and separate from sinners (Hebrews 7:26). With the church it is separation in the sense of being set apart for God's own possession, to be His people, His property, His pleasure and His servants. It is that separation which is seen to be inevitable when the intentions of God are grasped. God desires and determines to dwell in the midst of His people, and this makes the church holy ground and we must never forget it.

Last of all, the church is *sent* in the name of, and by the authority of, God through the whole wide world to do His will, to be His witnesses, and to show forth the praises of Him who has called His people out of darkness into His marvellous light (1 Peter 2:9).

The church is by definition a crusading church, an advancing church, a church with its eyes on the ultimate victory. We are led along in Christ's triumphal procession (2 Corinthians 2:14). Christ Himself has declared that *He* will build His church and the gates of hell shall not prevail against it. Many a time the church stands surrounded by the stormy seas of experience; often she is scarcely recognisable as the church; but she cannot be stopped, let alone destroyed. Today we have the noise of battle, but the next we shall sing the victor's song, because the victory is Christ's and that victory has been given to us.

> 'Crowns and thrones may perish,
> Kingdoms rise and wane,
> But the church of Jesus,

Constant will remain;
Gates of hell can never
    'Gainst that church prevail;
We have Christ's own promise,
    And that cannot fail.
Onward! Christian soldiers,
    Marching as to war,
With the cross of Jesus
    Going on before' (S. Baring - Gould).

CHAPTER THIRTEEN

THE COMMUNION OF SAINTS

The final section of the Apostles' Creed contains brief but trenchant phrases. Having spoken of God the Father and God the Son in the glory of His work of redemption, the Creed goes on to say, 'I believe in the Holy Ghost, the Holy Catholic Church, the Communion of Saints.' This third phrase, the Communion of Saints, follows on closely from the doctrine of the church.

In considering the church we emphasised the essential fundamental spiritual unity in Christ of all believers. If we are in Christ we are in the true church, and if we are in the church, we are inevitably and inescapably united together with all other believing men and women who rest their souls' salvation and their eternal hope in the crucified, risen Son of God. That being so, the whole business of what we call the Ecumenical Movement is in one sense unnecessary. It is seeking to bring into being what is already a spiritual fact. All who are in Christ are one in Christ, and if we depart from that glorious truth, and seek to engineer something of an ecclesiastical colossus in which the admixture of faith and unbelief is almost beyond expression, then we have departed altogether from God. The doctrine of the church leads on to the theme of the communion of saints. After all, if the resurrection of Christ signifies victory over death, then the mere fact of death cannot possible separate one believer from other believers, whether in this world or the next.

We have emphasised that religion must be personal. But we will never deal fully or faithfully with Christ if we keep ourselves to ourselves and try to go it alone. The Bible knows nothing at all about Christians who isolate themselves by choice, but makes it very plain that we need each other, not merely because we desire each other's Christian company but because we *need* each other if we are going to be real Christians. We need each other if we are going to be now, and to become in the future, all that God purposes for us. This theme of the commonly shared life of believers is taken up in the phrase, 'the communion of saints'.

At once we face two words that are prone to be misunderstood, 'communion' and 'saints'. To many people, especially church people in Scotland, communion signifies a service you come to quarterly, or half-yearly, a formal religious occasion, vested in many sentimental minds with a significance that is thoroughly unbiblical. People whose interest in the things of Christ is minimal justify themselves to each other and to their minister by saying, 'At least I come to communion,' as if by some process of spiritual magic this kept them right with God. Such people forget that the Bible says quite clearly that if we come to a communion service and eat and drink the bread and the wine in an attitude that is unworthy, with unbelieving hearts, then we eat and drink judgment, not merely to our souls, but to our lives (1 Corinthians 11:27 ff). It is evident in some churches on a Communion Sunday that the last thing in the world that many of the congregation are experiencing is what is meant by the word 'communion', a meeting with and fellowship with God. For many it is mere formality. This is not the communion we speak of.

The other word 'saints' is also devalued in our modern vocabulary. It conjures up a picture of very pious people, possibly with haloes and a strange unworldly look. Such people are unreal, and very unlike Jesus Christ because He was a totally human man who would call a spade a spade, to the extent that He trampled on many toes and made countless enemies. The word 'saints' has come to signify well-meaning religious people who are so heavenly minded that they are no earthly use; but this is not what the Bible means when it uses the word 'saints'. One child defined a saint as a dead clergyman! Another child, thinking in terms of the stained glass windows in a church, got nearer the point when he said a saint is a man that you can see through. That is getting near the meaning of 'saint'.

Using that illustration of the stained glass window, we could say that a saint is someone through whom the light of God shines to men. The Bible says that we who have believed in the name of Jesus Christ unto salvation are called to be saints, to be the kind of men and women through whose lives the very light of God can shine to lighten the darkness of men. We all know a window is something through which the light should shine, but a window can be very dirty and thus be ineffective and indeed a hindrance to light. Many of the 'saints' of God are sorely in need of a heavenly window cleaner, so that they might become that for which they have been saved in the salvation of God. How else can we let our light shine (Matthew 5:16)?

This word 'saint' in the Bible does not describe the actual moral or spiritual condition of the Christian, as if the saint was in some sense the honours graduate of the spiritual university. It is more basic than that. Saints are ordinary people, in every place, in every level of society, from every intellectual, educational and social background, who are set apart to belong to God in Jesus Christ. If you belong to God through Jesus Christ, then you are a saint. Saints are people who have heard the gospel, the good news of the grace of God in Jesus Christ, the mighty and magnificent offer of salvation and life that is eternal in all its full unfettered quality, and they have believed. The word of the gospel awakened a sense of need, desire and hunger in their hearts and they responded. They professed the name of Christ, and they know themselves now to have been laid hold upon by God and for God. These are the 'saints'.

Inevitably and instinctively, by the constraint of the Spirit such people come together, and they become in any given city, village, factory, university, neighbourhood, a colony of heaven. They are men and women whose life is eternal life. They are not the same as the people around them. They are *in Christ*. They do not belong to this world any more. They are strangers and pilgrims with a heavenly destiny (Hebrews 11:13 AV). When you go to a new city you seek out the people who are set upon following Christ, and right from the start, making allowance for certain personality clashes and temperamental differences (which are essentially superficial and can be overcome with effort) you find yourself *in fellowship* with these people. You belong to them, and they belong to you. This is the communion of the saints. You have never met before, but the moment you come together and discover you are both in Christ, and belong to Christ, and desire Christ, and serve Christ, then you are in fellowship. If this is not so, there is something wrong with your Christianity.

When I began to study this theme I found myself thinking of the very first time I attended a communion service, having been converted as a seaman in the Royal Navy during the war. In Singapore I went ashore with one or two friends who took me to a meeting place of Christians. I can picture it now. There were people of all colours and backgrounds, from many different nations, but I knew I belonged. I think the man on my left was a Malay, and one sitting on the other side was Chinese. Although I did not fully understand the sermon that was preached, and felt a little strange in the particular form of the communion service, yet the fact remained: I belonged. I belonged to them because I belonged to Christ. I experienced something of the communion of saints.

The meaning of the communion of saints cannot stop there, because from time to time those we have come to love and with whom we have shared a common life must go elsewhere. People are transferred, and it can be very sore when it seems that God is taking people away from the fellowship where they are valued and needed; but, of course, the saints belong to God, not to us, and the whole purpose of their being under a biblical ministry is that they might be prepared to be sent out into the world to be the windows through which the light of God can shine to men. Separation in service comes, but such is the nature of our fellowship, this communion of saints, this fundamental belonging together, that neither geographical distance nor lapse of time can possible break it. There is a hymn that says:

'Blest be the tie that binds
Our hearts in Jesus' love;
The fellowship of Christian minds
Is like to that above' (Fawcett).

One of the thrills of Christian life and service is the awareness of being one with so many of God's people scattered throughout the world. We cannot but anticipate the greater thrill that will be ours when we are gathered together in glory.

If this fellowship, this unbreakable communion, defies geographical location, it also defies the bounds of time. Even death itself cannot break it. We Christians have scarcely begun to take a realistic view of death and heaven. For a Christian, death, sad and grievous as it is, must be kept within the perspective of faith. In a real sense it is insignificant: it cannot do anything permanent. It can neither separate us from Christ nor essentially separate us from our brothers and sisters in Christ. If the fellowship we speak about is something that extends its mighty sway horizontally, throughout the geography of the whole world, it is also a fellowship that operates and binds vertically, so that we can dispose of what some call 'the great divide' between this world and the world to come. Of course we have no intention at all of having any dealings with what is called 'spiritualism', but the fact remains that inasmuch as we are not separated from one another here, neither are we separated from those above. Think of those dear Christians with whom we have worshipped, prayed and served, whose earthly lives are over and who have been 'promoted to glory'. How we loved being with them! Do we now suggest for a moment that some great destructive scythe has cut through the fellowship that we enjoyed with them so that they are lost to us for ever? Our attitude is different from that.

> 'Therefore, since we are surrounded by so great a cloud of witnesses, let us also lay aside every weight, and sin which clings so closely, and let us run with perseverance the race that is set before us' (Hebrews 12:1).

Think of those Christians who have now many of their loved ones in heaven. Think of how, as the years go past, the number of saints gathered in heaven is increasing until we cannot help but think that soon the balance will tip over, and time as we know it will give place to eternity. Think of the story of Moses and Elijah, who appeared with Christ on the Mount of Transfiguration, talking in earnest and informed tones of the work that Jesus was about to do on the cross (Luke 9:31). Moses and Elijah had left this earthly scene so long before, but they were

160

right up-to-date with what was happening on earth and they were still sharing in the ongoing work of God. Christians criticise the materialistic spirit of the world but we tend to be terribly blighted by it ourselves. So much of our thinking is solidly anchored in the business of earth that we forget the reality and nearness of the world that is to come. Every day as we live our lives we are far nearer eternity than we realise. The 'world to come' is not a great distance away. The separation is not so radical as we sometimes think and feel. When you think of all the glorified saints of God in heaven, these men and women who have fought, suffered and died for Christ and the gospel and have carried their battle scars into the presence of God, can you not think of them as just through a thin wall? We become aware of them, and of their awareness of us; we begin to realise our participation with them and theirs with us. This is the fellowship, the communion of the saints. And what a fellowship it is! We are to be pitied indeed if our lives are conditioned by and lived only on the basis of those things that are seen and temporal. If that is our life we are poor indeed.

Bring this whole broad theme to its practical application. Remember that sin always has a divisive and disruptive effect that casts us out from the vital centre to the perimeter, whereas the grace of God counteracts the effect of sin and brings us together again. Think of this as it is expressed in 1 John 1:1-9. In the seventh verse there are three phrases relevant to the theme of the communion or fellowship of the saints. 'If we walk in the light,' 'we have fellowship,' and 'the blood of Jesus Christ, God's Son, keeps on cleansing us from all sin.'

What does it mean to walk in the light? It means that we stop being a 'shady' character in relation to God and to people. It is not a case of wearing our hearts on our sleeves, showing everyone everything we think or feel. There is no call for making public those things that are rightly private and personal. But there is a tendency to be too secretive, too calculating in what we say and how we say it. At times we can talk at length with someone, and afterwards become aware that there has been no real communication, no openness, no sharing and, of course, no fellowship. Because we have not been open we do not know each other. That is walking in the shadows, not in the light. To walk in the light means there must be no concealment, and no need to try to conceal, because in fact there is nothing to hide. It is a great relief when you have nothing to hide. It puts a spring into your step. Years ago, in the Ruanda revival in Africa, the catchword was 'walking in the light'. These Africans were saying to each other, 'Brother, I want to walk in the light with you.' Things came out into the open and were put right. If we walk in the light we have fellowship.

We must also walk in the light with God, out in the open with Him, honest with Him, so living in His presence that His light enables us to see ourselves and others in true perspective. The ninth verse in the passage from John speaks about confessing our sins. There is no substitute for prompt confession to God, and to men, even though our natural reaction is to hold back and to go on as if nothing had happened. David did that after his great sin, and he speaks about that in Psalm 32. When he kept silent about his sin and refused to confess it, the whole of his inward personality dried up. He found himself shut off from his fellows. He was alone. Sin does that, therefore sin has to be confessed. But keep in mind that to *admit* something is not the same as to *confess* it. When we admit something we try to explain it: we give a whole list of reasons why it happened; we make excuses because of our personality; we call it weakness. *That* is not confessing. To confess something is to name it as your own, then to let it go, and cast it away from you. To fail to confess sin is to put yourself out of reach of the cleansing virtue of the death of Christ; but if we confess our sins the blood of Jesus Christ cleanses and keeps on cleansing us from our sins. Being 'clean' we have fellowship with God and with one another.

The Greek word for fellowship is 'koinonia', and speaks of a quality of association in which time is forgotten, something that almost lifts you into a different dimension. You get a taste of it sometimes when you have friends in your home for an evening. The fellowship (you may not consciously call it that) is so real that the evening flies on, and then somebody suddenly says, 'Is that the time already?' Time had ceased to be: for a spell you were lifted out of time. This is fellowship. If we keep company with Jesus we have fellowship like that. Of course a group of Christians together does not necessarily mean that there is fellowship. You can gather together a group of Christians and find they are in a state of what is almost underground warfare, a cold war of nerves and tension. For various reasons, often past hurts and disappointments, people can be on the defensive, and their attitude in relationships is one of 'keep your distance.' Fear of some kind is dominant, and there can be no real fellowship. But the love of God in Jesus Christ can cast out fear (1 John 4:18) and we begin to relax. We become aware that we are accepted in Christ, and fellowship can begin and be enjoyed.

If we walk in the light we have fellowship, but if we do not walk in the light we have no fellowship. When we have no fellowship with God there is no joy, and there is no witness. Read Acts 2:46,47. What fellowship there was, what common life they shared, what joy bubbled up amongst them! If ever Christians got excited about Jesus it was then, and with great power they witnessed, and the Lord added to the church daily such as were being saved.

If we walk in the light we have fellowship, but if in our hearts and lives there are sins unconfessed, prejudices and suspicions harboured, plans made that are not of God, positions in respect of the things of God that we no longer hold, we are not walking in the light, we are shady characters, and we have no fellowship. If we walk in the light we have fellowship, and the blood of Jesus Christ, God's own Son, keeps on progressively, increasingly, pushing its way into every avenue of our life and personality to further the work of sanctification, making our sainthood a reality. When we speak of the blood of Jesus Christ, we speak of all the power of the saving death of Jesus Christ on the cross, not only for forgiveness but for the sanctification of our whole life and character, taking every disposition of our personalities and moulding all in a way that will bring pleasure to God.

We need to ask ourselves if we are in fact experiencing the joy of fellowship with God and with our God-given brothers and sisters. Is the great grace of God in Jesus Christ going on with its work in our lives and personalities, changing our thinking, thought-forms, feelings, actions, desires, motives and relationships?

The Bible speaks of lepers being cleansed. In one particular incident we are told of how the withered, decayed flesh of the leper came again like the flesh of a little child, clean, unmarked, firm and healthy (2 Kings 5:14). God can do that for our lives and personalities. When He does it, and as He goes on doing it, He brings us together into the fellowship, the communion of the saints.

CHAPTER FOURTEEN

THE FORGIVENESS OF SINS

The church of Jesus Christ is not a vague association of people with tendencies towards religion and humanitarianism, because you can have these particular 'diseases' without being remotely connected to Jesus Christ. I deliberately call them diseases because that is what they can be. You can be so preoccupied with religion that Jesus Christ has no place at all, and you can be so bemused by humanitarian doctrines, so concerned with humanity at large, that you have not time to be interested in the people next door. The church of Jesus Christ is a company of forgiven sinners who may rightly be called saints, ordinary men and women set apart by God and for God in and through the salvation that is in Christ. Having found salvation in Him they enjoy fellowship together in the power of the gospel, being aware of the fact that they are called to an eternal and heavenly destiny of glory.

Such a definition of the church can lend itself to hypocrisy. It is easy for those who know the truth of the saving grace of God in Jesus Christ to become like the Pharisees and feel that, having been laid hold upon by God, they are in some way superior people. Such persons, not necessarily openly in words, but certainly in their hearts, tend to pray that prayer of the Pharisee that is so totally unacceptable to God, 'I thank Thee God, that I am not like other men' (Luke 18:11). This is something to be guarded against. We must set the highest standards both morally and spiritually for those who call themselves by the name of Christ, standards that can never be qualified. Yet at the same time we must never deny the fact that there is forgiveness with God for those

165

who fail and fall: a forgiveness that is so rich, majestic and staggering in its concept that it takes the whole of the Bible to expound it. The forgiveness of God is full, free, total, absolute and immediate towards men and women, even when their sins have been deliberate and repeated. God takes men and women who have neither excuse nor justification for their sins, shows them what they really are, calls them to repentance and says there is forgiveness. Little wonder David the Psalmist cried out in relief after he had, by painful experience, been brought to acknowledge, confess and repent of his great sin, 'O the blessedness of the man whose sins are forgiven' (Psalm 32:1).

This fact, forgiveness shown to the undeserving needs the whole Bible to expound it. It is found, for example, in the prophets. God looked on the sins of His people, recognising that righteousness demands judgment. Then God said:

'How can I give you up, O Ephraim? ....
I will heal their faithlessness; I will love them freely, for My anger has turned from them' (Hosea 11:8, 14:4).

'Come now, let us reason together, says the Lord: though your sins are like scarlet, they shall be as white as snow; though they are red like crimson, they shall become like wool' (Isaiah 1:18).

Whatever we mean by the word 'saint' or the word 'Christian' however much we are able to grasp the glorious thing that God has done for us in Jesus Christ, we must never forget that we are only and always sinners saved by grace. If we remembered this our hearts would be guarded against pride and our tongues would largely be drained of the venom of criticism of others. The words of Jesus would always be in our hearts, 'Let him who is without sin, cast the first stone' (John 8:7).

This subject of forgiveness is difficult to grasp because we know so little of it. Forgiveness is something that we find very difficult to give or to receive. It is easy to shrug off some slight annoyance, but if someone has really hurt us, cutting deeply into our feelings, it is tremendously difficult to forgive. In our better moments we are apt to say, 'Because I am a Christian I think I can forgive, but I doubt if I can ever forget.' That is not biblical forgiveness.

Forgiveness is difficult to give but also to accept. When we know that we have done wrong to someone who did not deserve it, and then become aware that they bear us no grudge, that they are not going to make any difference to the relationship because as far as they are concerned it is all forgiven and consigned to the past, we find it difficult to accept. We would feel better if we paid some penalty or penance. We do not like being in that kind of debt. There are times when we are tempted to say that we can forgive others but not ourselves. That is a form of pride. It assumes that our sins are greater and fuller than anyone else's, too great for God to forgive.

Our thoughts of forgiveness are so shallow and mixed up that we tend to think in terms of letting people off. When we think like that we soon have very weak and strange ideas about punishment, and erroneous ideas about sin itself. We stop using the word 'sin' and we talk about weakness, environment and social pressures. The result is the strange and disturbing situation in which we now live. Men are sent to prison, having left a trail of hurt, destruction and death behind them, and there is a cry of protest from the social reformers saying that this is barbarism and dehumanises those incarcerated. The emphasis is not one of concern for the poor people who have been done to death, nor for their families, but

167

concern for the criminal, regardless of his crime.

The Bible is not confused when it talks about sin, and from the opening chapters of Genesis right through to the closing chapters of the Book of Revelation the message is written clear and plain. First of all the Bible says that sin is punished; of that there is no doubt. Sin is also forgiven; that too is clear and plain in the Bible. Sin is also something that has consequences, both temporal and eternal, that is, consequences in this life and in the life to come. In the lives of believers and unbelievers sin has consequences that cannot be escaped. A poem, admittedly of little literary quality, speaks of how the bird with the broken wing never flies so high again. Sin does have consequences. Even within the magnificent forgiveness of God, and all that forgiveness means in terms of restoration to the home and the fellowship of the Father, there is an aftermath. There is a residue of sin, an entail or sediment of sin, sometimes a lifelong scar, tension or regret in the person, the character, the body and the very soul of the sinner. Yet all these facts do not in any sense whatever contradict or qualify one of the most amazing statements ever made about Jesus, a statement made by His enemies, 'This man receives sinners.'

Read about this in Luke 15:1-6:

> 'Now the tax collectors and sinners were all drawing near to hear Him. And the Pharisees and the scribes murmured, saying, "This man receives sinners and eats with them." '

These men proud of their religious standing and pedigree would not do that. They considered they had more respect for their personal sanctity than to act so; more respect for the temple of God and for the judgment of the law of God than to do such a thing. And Jesus spoke this parable to them, saying:

'What man of you, having a hundred sheep, if he has lost one of them, does not leave the ninety-nine in the wilderness, and go after the one which is lost, until he finds it? And when he has found it, he lays it on his shoulders, rejoicing. And when he comes home, he calls together his friends and his neighbours, saying to them, "Rejoice with me, for I have found my sheep which was lost." '

That is God's attitude to sinners. He was looking for them, recognising that their stupidity had led to their being lost, and being aware that like lost sheep they would probably be frightened. Can you imagine God rejoicing over a restored sinner described in such devastating terms as we read in Isaiah 1:1-15 and Romans 1:18-32? Think of men and women who have plumbed the depths of iniquity, and see God the mighty Saviour in Jesus Christ scouring the face of the earth looking for them! Can you imagine men and angels looking at God and asking, 'What are You hunting for with such earnestness?' Then eventually in some gutter or derelict place, some place of licence and corruption, God finds the sheep that is lost and the angels can tell from the look on His face that He has found priceless treasure. Is that what God was looking for? God says, 'Rejoice with Me; for I have found My sheep that was lost.'

Think now of the story of the Prodigal Son in Luke 15:11 ff:

'And he said, "There was a man who had two sons; and the younger of them said to his father, 'Father, give me the share of property that falls to me.' And he divided his living between them. Not many days later, the younger son gathered all he had and took his journey into a far country, and there he squandered his property in loose living. And when he had spent everything, a great famine arose in that country, and he began to be in want. So he went and joined himself to one of the citizens of that country, who sent him into his fields to feed swine. And he would gladly have fed on the pods that the swine ate; and no-one gave him anything. But when he came to himself he said, 'How many of my father's hired servants have bread enough and to spare, but I perish here with hunger! I will arise and go to my father, and I will say to him, "Father, I have sinned against heaven and before you; I am no longer worthy to be called your son; treat me as one of your hired servants." And he arose and came to his father.......'

The far country with its separation and shame gives a picture of what sin does. Remember what the young lad had been and had now become. The life he had chosen had gone sour on him. Think not only of the rags and tatters of his clothing and his body, but the torn shreds of his mind, emotions and spirit. The whole of his personality was blasted and blighted, and no doubt there was shame.

'But while he was yet at a distance his father (who had never stopped loving, and must have been looking and waiting) saw him and had compassion, and ran and embraced him and kissed him. (Remember the tatters and the dirt; the stench, the brokenness, and the sores of corruption.) And the son said to him, "Father, I have sinned against heaven and before you; I am no longer worthy to be called your son." But the father said to his servants, "Bring quickly the best robe, and put it on him; and put a ring on his hand, and shoes on his feet; and bring the fatted calf and kill it, and let us eat and make merry; for this my son was dead, and is alive again; he was lost, and is found.....″ ′

That is the forgiveness of sins. It is quite astonishing. It is all about the God who takes you back when you have nothing to say for yourself, no means of justifying yourself, and no excuses to make for yourself. You stand in all the rags of your sinnerhood, and in the moment your heart compels your eyes to look towards your Father, He sees, and He *runs*. One preacher summarised the story of the Prodigal: Sick of home; Home-sick; Home! Forgiveness and home are two wonderful words.

The wonder of forgiveness comes home to our hearts only when we begin to realise something of what sin is and what sin does. What is sin? The Shorter Catechism answers: 'Sin is any want of conformity unto or transgression of the law of God.' The word 'sin' itself is a word that speaks of falling short, or going too far, or going off the straight. It is what you see when rolling a bowl along a bowling green towards the jack. Sometimes it falls short, sometimes goes too far, sometimes goes off to the side, drawn by its inbuilt bias. Several different words are used in the Bible to show what sin is and study of these makes plain that it is far more than just acts of wrong-doing. Sin is something dynamic; it is like a virus; it is active and progressive, like a sickness that can go through the whole of the personality inflaming it and ultimately bringing it to death, if it is not checked. Sin works all sorts of damage to mind, heart, body and soul and its final effect is death (James 1:15).

Consider briefly some of the words the Bible uses for sin. The word 'sin' itself speaks of missing the mark and we are told that all have sinned and fall short (Romans

3:23). The world 'transgression' signifies stepping across, going out of bounds, and it carries with it the idea of guilt, because we know that we should not have done so. It is sometimes deliberate and sometimes as a result of neglect and lack of watchfulness. It is both negative and positive and things not done can be sin just as much as things done. 'If a man knows what is right and fails to do it, his failure is sin' (James 4:17. JBP). People asked Jesus on one occasion, 'What must we do, to be doing the work of God?' And Jesus said, 'This is the work of God, that you believe in Him whom He has sent' (John 6:28,29). That is what God wants us to do, come to Jesus, and it is our failure to come to Jesus that constitutes our greatest sin.

A further word to denote sin and reveal its nature is 'iniquity', which signifies a distortion or a perversion at the very heart of the personality. It is not so much the act of sin that is spoken of here as the nature and attitude of the sinner. I have been trying to find a word to convey this thought of iniquity and the only one I can think of is 'cussedness'. Being a parent is quite an education. You find your child doing something he knows is wrong, and you rebuke him, saying for example, 'Don't put your dirty hands on the wallpaper!' Now, even when you are rebuking the child, and he is looking up at you with eyes that seem to denote absolute concentration, you may well see the child's hand going out just to draw a finger along the wallpaper. That is 'cussedness', or iniquity. We know full well we can look into the face of God, with eyes that seem to indicate obedience and devotion, and all the time our hearts are already set on going after sin. Little wonder the Bible says that the heart of man is hopelessly diseased (Jeremiah 17:9). It is because we are sinners by nature that we show ourselves to be sinners by choice and practice.

Sin is also 'rebellion'. This is lawlessness, deliberate refusal to do the will of God, the kind of thing we read of in Romans 1:18 ff. It is the attitude of mind and heart that is nothing less than the dethronement of God and the enthronement of self. It is the attitude or disposition expressed in the words of Pharaoh when he said in defiance, 'Who is the Lord that I should obey His voice?' (Exodus 5:2 AV). It signifies those of whom it is said, 'God is not in all his thoughts' (Psalms 10:4 AV), and 'there is no fear of God before their eyes' (Psalms 36:1; Romans 3:18). It is the attitude of God-rejection that leads to a society in which every man does what is right in his own eyes (Judges 21:25). The spirit of lawlessness is one of the most frightening aspects of modern society and it leads to fear and destruction.

The final word for sin which we consider speaks of 'wickedness', and indicates the state a man is left in as a result of sin. Having considered what sin is, think now of what sin does. All we have said brings home to the heart the truth of Scripture when it says that all have sinned and have come short of the glory of God. But what does sin do? These words of Robert Burns in a poem that is entitled 'Epistle to a Young Friend' seem to answer the question:

> 'I waive the quantum o' the sin,
> The hazard of concealing;
> But och! it hardens a' within,
> And petrifies the feeling!'

Sin: it hardens and petrifies, making the heart hard as stone.

The Bible uses three illustrations to bring this home. It speaks of the sinner as being a leper, and all through the Bible leprosy symbolises a dread sickness of the soul, which neither man nor medicine can cure. To be a sinner means to be a victim, struck down by the dread disease that spreads through the whole of your life and devours you. The illustration is a vivid one in today's sick society.

The Bible also speaks of the sinner as being a prisoner. Nowhere is the stupidity and pride of men more manifest than when they say, 'It does me no harm.' They say, 'I know when to stop,' and 'It is all a matter of moderation.' But when they try to stop they find out how trapped they are! Think of the power of drink, drugs, and tobacco, to name but a few areas of problem.

> 'Sow a thought, reap an action. Sow an action reap a habit. Sow a habit, reap a character. Sow a character, reap a destiny.'

Sin is not something we can play with. Jesus said, 'Truly, truly, I say to you, every one who commits sin is a slave to sin' (John 8:34). A simple illustration brings it home clearly. Having your arms tied to your side by a single strand of white cotton thread does not make you a prisoner. You can break the thread easily. Wind it round a couple of times and you can still break it. But take that thin thread and wind it round and round many times (try the experiment) and it is not long before you *are* a prisoner!

Lastly, from the beginning to the end of the Bible we are shown (and how frightening it is to see it) that to be a sinner means to be an enemy of God. Recall the story of the Garden of Eden. What happened after our first parents sinned and the conviction of sin came upon their hearts and the word of God concerning their sin was spoken? They were excluded from the paradise of God! They were put out from His presence. An angel messenger of God with a flaming sword was set at the gate guarding the way to life, and no sinner could ever re-enter. The wrath of God is revealed against all ungodliness and wickedness of men (Romans 1:18). It is revealed not only in the Scriptures but all through the pages of history, and in a climactic way in the cross of Calvary, where the judgment of God fell upon human sin.

We have considered what sin is and what it does. Now what is the remedy?

We deal with this in a deliberately brief way because it is not a difficult or drawn-out process for God to forgive. We do not make light of the price that was paid on the cross. It was indeed an infinitely costly salvation. But for the sake of His Son who loved us and gave Himself for us, God forgives. We see the glory of it in the story of the Prodigal, when the father ran to meet the penitent, returning son. Is there any other instance in the Bible of God being shown as running?

What then is forgiveness? It is that great action of God in Jesus Christ that reverses the whole situation of sin for those who come in faith to Jesus Christ. The guilty are forgiven; the leper is healed; the prisoner is set free; the enemy is reconciled. There are many wonderful words used in the Bible for forgiveness. To forgive means to hide the sin, to get rid of the sin, to leave sin behind, to forget, to blot out, to cancel. To be forgiven means to be washed, to be saved, to be delivered, to be healed from sickness, to be restored to the Father's home and service. That is the forgiveness of sins.

There is a story, no doubt apocryphal, of a man who used to disturb a preacher by shouting out, 'Hallelujah!' Eventually the preacher struck on a bright idea and gave the man an encyclopedia to read during the sermon. This kept him very quiet for a long time, until on one occasion during a sermon there came from this man a mighty 'Hallelujah!' Afterwards the minister demanded an explanation, and the man, looking a bit crestfallen said, 'Sir, I could not help it. I was reading in the encyclopedia about the Pacific Ocean and it told me the immense depth of the ocean at one particular point. I was thinking about this and remembered that the Bible says that God has taken my sins and cast them into the depths of the sea. I just had to say "Hallelujah!" ' Do you blame him? Should we not thrill with excitement and wonder when we think of the forgiveness of all our sins?

God says,

> 'For I will be merciful towards their iniquities. And I will remember their sins no more' (Hebrews 8:12).

That is forgiveness. That is what the prodigal discovered when the arms of his father were round about him, when the rags were taken off, and the best robe was put on, and the ring of sonship and the shoes of service were put upon his feet. Can you imagine the prodigal saying in his heart, when the party was over and he was back in his own room in his father's house; 'It is all past. My sins are all forgiven.'

To impress on our hearts the wonder of God's forgiveness ponder with awe these Scriptures:

> 'Do you not know the unrighteous will not inherit the kingdom of God? Do not be deceived; neither the immoral, nor idolators, nor adulterers, nor homosexuals, nor thieves, nor the greedy, nor drunkards, nor revilers, nor robbers will inherit the kingdom of God. And such were some of you. But you were washed, you were sanctified, you were justified in the name of the Lord Jesus Christ and in the Spirit of our God' (1 Corinthians 6:9-11).

> 'Blessed is he whose transgression is forgiven, whose sin is covered' (Psalm 32:1).

CHAPTER FIFTEEN

THE RESURRECTION OF THE BODY

It is always a good thing to come to grips with the doctrines of the Christian faith. It brings into focus and emphasises that there are certain facts and propositions about God, Christ, life and death that Christians believe, stand upon and refuse to yield. We hold to the historic faith that was once for all delivered to the saints (Jude 3). As we have studied these successive statements of the Apostles' Creed we have seen that the message of the Christian gospel is in fact relevant and provides a contemporary answer to the hunger and seeking of human hearts. When everything is in a state of flux, when no one seems to be sure about anything, when no one seems prepared to state categorical truths, we have the great affirmation of faith in the Creed: 'I believe ....'. We have a message of sufficient calibre to go out into a world of uncertainty, a world that has lost the meaning, the purpose, the direction and the foundation of life. This is the message we proclaim on the basis of facts we have heard, believed and proved to be true.

In the fundamental doctrines of the faith we have the message that meets the present cry of the human heart. This is certainly true when we declare that we believe in the resurrection of the body. We must be quite clear in our thinking about this. The Bible makes it perfectly plain that if there is no resurrection then there is nothing and the whole of the Christian gospel collapses and is a sham (1 Corinthians 15:13-17). Everything folds up on us; we are left with little more than sheer animal life, to eat, drink and be merry, for tomorrow we die (1 Corinthians 15:32).

We have in earlier chapters considered the

statements concerning Jesus Christ, to the effect that He descended into hell and the third day rose again from the dead. The main emphasis has been on the victory of Jesus Christ over sin, death, the grave, hell and all that we mean by the powers of the kingdom of darkness. This is the victory which is given to us in Christ to be proved in the daily routine of life in a wicked and godless world. We ought to remind ourselves of this, first thing every morning, saying, 'Thanks be to God who gives us the victory through our Lord Jesus Christ' (1 Corinthians 15:57). If we did this more often our lives would be more marked by victory over the circumstances that so often hem us in and bring us to moral and spiritual defeat. The emphasis in this study is not so much on the resurrection of Christ as upon *our* resurrection, and in both cases we are speaking of the resurrection of *the body*, not just some 'spiritual' resurrection.

The one thing all can be sure about is that we shall die. This is the inescapable fact of experience. But the resurrection from the dead is a subject concerning which a great deal of confusion exists. People say, 'You live your life, you die, and that is that. There is nothing else, nothing more.' If that is what people believe we can understand in measure why some seek to escape from reality by getting drunk. If this is the philosophy of life we have passed on to the younger generation we cannot wholly blame them for taking drugs to try to get a sensuous trip into another kind of world.

Other people talk about what they call 'conditional immortality', suggesting that some people with a certain kind of faith have hope of immortality and a happy life beyond the grave but others face annihilation. Others again have a philosophy of life expressed in terms of reincarnation. You come into this world, live and die and, depending on the success or otherwise of your life, somehow or other you come back again and live another life in another form, not necessarily human, and not necessarily better than the one before. Some people live their lives on the basis of what we would call 'spiritism' with all its communications, apparitions and messages, which are not *all* a hoax, and are dangerous.

All these philosophies are essentially non-substantial. There is nothing in them to get a grip on in this life and even less to get a sure grip on regarding the life that is to come. But the Christian message is quite clear: we believe in the resurrection of the body. The world to come is real and substantial. We must not think of heaven as a place of disembodied spirits floating about in a condition of ethereal bliss! That has no appeal, and, more importantly, has no basis in the Bible.

The Christian message concerns the resurrection of the body. Recall the words of Jesus:

'Do not marvel at this; for the hour is coming when all who are in the tombs will hear His voice and come forth, those who have done good, to the resurrection of life, and those who have done evil, to the resurrection of judgment' (John 5:28,29).

This speaks of a real bodily resurrection of those who have died in faith and those who have died in unbelief. We quote the words of Job, although there is much debate as to what the true translation is:

'I know that my Redeemer lives, and that in the end He will stand upon the earth. And after my skin has been destroyed, yet in my flesh I will see God' (Job 19:25,26 NIV).

We add Paul's statement from 1 Corinthians 15:35-44:

'But some one will ask, "How are the dead raised? With what kind of body do they come?"

You foolish man! What you sow does not come to life unless it dies. And what you sow is not the body which is to be, but a bare kernel, perhaps of wheat or of some other grain. But God gives it a body as He has chosen, and to each kind of seed its own body. For not all flesh is alike, but there is one kind for men, another for animals, another for birds, and another for fish. There are celestial bodies and there are terrestrial bodies; but the glory of the celestial is one, and the glory of the terrestrial is another. There is one glory of the sun, and another glory of the moon, and another glory of the stars; for star differs from star in glory.

So it is with the resurrection of the dead. What is sown is perishable, what is raised is imperishable. It is sown in dishonour, it is raised in glory. It is sown in weakness, it is raised in power. It is sown a physical body, it is raised a spiritual body. If there is a physical body, there is also a spiritual body.'

It is clear that Paul envisages a resurrection body that is positively related to the present physical body and yet is different: not in the sense that it is less real than our present body, rather that it is the fulfilment or full-grown expression of what we are now, just as the full-grown corn is different from and greater than the mere seed. However difficult it may be to grasp such a truth we must see that our resurrection is not an allegorical or spiritualised one. The Christian believes in the resurrection of the body.

Consider also the demonstration of the power of Jesus Christ over death in the story of Lazarus (John 11:1ff). Jesus' very good friend had died, and the two sisters, Mary and Martha, and quite a company of others, together with Jesus went to the grave, which was a cave dug in the rock with a boulder rolled up to seal it. Jesus ordered them to take away the stone. The people were shocked, protesting that the body would be already at the stage of physical decomposition. We have no reason to doubt that that was in fact the case. Earlier Jesus had said:

> 'I am the resurrection and the life; he who believes in Me, though he die, yet shall he live, and whoever lives and believes in Me shall never die' (John 11:25,26).

Jesus called out in a loud voice (not for Lazarus' sake but for the sake of the crowd, that they might all hear), 'Lazarus, come out!' and the dead man came out bodily from his grave.

The resurrection of the body is a doctrine which cannot be grasped apart from the work of Christ and the power of Christ. In the risen Christ we see a true and recognisable man complete in body and personality. Remember that He ate a meal with the disciples (Luke 24:41-43, John 21:9-14). And that Man, risen from the dead, is even now in the presence of God the Father Almighty. People may mock and laugh at any concept of 'God up there' or 'heaven up there'. But there is a *Man* with a resurrection body in heaven. Remember, there was no body left in the tomb when Jesus rose from the dead. It was a physical bodily resurrection not a ghost (Luke 24:39). And our resurrection is a resurrection of the body, like His.

Why must there be the resurrection of the body? Is Christianity not all to do with the soul? Our talk about 'souls' can be a bit unreal. We should talk about *people*. When you think about it, whether in this life or in the resurrection, you need a body. Look at a corpse, possible someone you have known and loved very dearly, and as you stand there you are tremendously aware that this is not the person you knew and loved, because the spirit is gone. Yet all we knew of that person, all we mean by that loved one's personality and spirit, we knew in terms of bodily expression.   Appearance, words, actions, mannerisms, capacities, influence, are the things that make up the person. But none of these expressions of personality, none of the expressions of the 'spirit' of a loved one is possible without some bodily form. If that be true now, in this very temporary limited world, how much more will it be the case in the world to come? If the human spirit *here* cannot be expressed without a body for this little span of a few short years, how much more is a body needed in the world to come?

The human spirit, the person, cannot be expressed understandably without a body. In the world to come we could never be ourselves simply as 'souls'. Think of it this way: some have pen-pals and over a long spell correspond with someone they have never set eyes on. By means of their letters they get to know each other, but only in a limited way. We do not really know people until we have met them 'in the flesh'. If we meet them when they are sick, or just recovering from a serious illness, we will get one kind of impression about the person. If we meet them when they are hale and hearty, in the full bloom of health, we will get another impression of them. The condition of the body is a vital factor. The body allows the expression and projection of the person. Without an effective body we can never be our true selves. If the real person is to be known in all his fullness, then there must be a body that has absolutely no limitation, capable of carrying and expressing all that the person is in Christ, first in this world, and then in the world to come. It has to be a spiritual body. And we have the promise in Philippians 3:21 that it will be a glorious body.

I have a painting in my house and the artist said of it, 'The frame doesn't do anything for it. It needs a different kind of frame.' Apply the illustration to the subject of the resurrection body. Get a frame conceived, planned and provided by God Himself, the great Artist. Put the 'painting', the 'person', into that specifically designed frame and you see it in its full glory. We need new bodies in heaven; our present bodies are no use to display all we are and have in Christ. When buying new hats or dresses, ladies look carefully in the mirror and say, 'No, I'll not have this one. It doesn't do anything for me.' They are looking for something carefully designed and wisely chosen in order to show forth personality as it really is.

The hymn that is a paraphrase of 1 John 3:1-4, says, 'What we shall hereafter be is hid from mortal eyes.' Even though we are born again of the Spirit of God, possessors of eternal life in Christ and indwelt by the Holy Spirit, this present bodily vehicle is not sufficient to express all that Christ has made us and has given to us. We need a new body, one without any limitation at all, that will be capable of carrying and expressing all that we are and shall be in Christ in the world that is to come. I know and love dearly the people in my congregation. Over the years I have found different aspects of their personalities, natures and characters tremendously interesting. When I think that in heaven all the inhibitions and limitations of mere worldly, earthly bodies will be gone, and they will be given new bodies so that all that they are in Christ will show to the full, I find the thought of heaven tremendously exciting.

The Christian gospel addresses itself to the whole of man, intellect, emotion, artistic and creative capacity, will, spirit, and body, so that what we mean by salvation is the salvation of the whole personality. If this salvation is ours, working out its fruit in our lives here in this world, then in the world to come the experience of life will be greater than here, not less. Too many people think of heaven as something of a consolation prize after they have had to leave this world. It is not! This world is the one of shadowy experience; the next is the real one. Too often we think of heaven as being a negation of this world, something totally detached from and independent of this world, this life, and these bodies. But it is not so.

Look at 2 Corinthians 5:1-10:

> 'We know that if the earthly tent we live in is destroyed (the word is the technical one that speaks of dismantling a tent, an operation which can be done with great rapidity, sometimes accidently in the middle of the night), we have a building (the tent is flimsy, non-substantial, the building is the reality, the permanent institution) from God, a house not made with hands, eternal in the heavens. Here indeed we groan and long to put on our heavenly dwelling, so that by putting it on we may not be found naked. For while we are still in this tent, we sigh with anxiety; not that we would be unclothed (we are not talking about escapism. This is not a case of Christians saying, "The world is a terrible place to be a Christian in:let's go away",) but that we would be further clothed, so that what is mortal (with all its limitations) may be swallowed up by life. He who has prepared us for this very thing is God, who has given us the Spirit (in our hearts) as a guarantee.
>
> So we are always of good courage; we know that while we are at home in the body we are away from the Lord .... We are of good courage, and

we would rather be away from the body (this flimsy tent) and at home with the Lord. So whether we are at home or away, we make it our aim to please Him. (We get down to the hard work of being Christians.) For we must all appear before the judgment seat of Christ, so that each one may receive good or evil, according to what he has done in the body.'

Paul is speaking of fulfilment. That is rather different from how people normally think about death. We speak, of course, of Christians, those who love the Lord, who trust the Lord for salvation. To them, death is fulfilment. Paul speaks here of death as an arrival, not a departure. People in the past used to talk about our 'dear departed'. That is not the way to talk about Christians: the dear ones have arrived. They are far better off than we are. They have become, as true men and women, all that they could be in Christ, all they could never be down here.

We are frustrated here with our limited minds, vocabularies, bodies and personalities, all shut up like valuables in safe-deposit in the vaults of a bank. One of the results of true preaching allied to pastoral care is that personalities should be 'opened up' by the name of God, and people set at liberty to be their true selves. This is life to the full as Jesus promised, 'I came that they may have life, and have it abundantly' (John 10:10). It can be ours in real measure now but in full expression only in the world to come.

Not only does Paul speak of death as an arrival, he speaks of a positive correlation between the bodily life here and now and that in the world to come. We 'receive the deeds done in the body', and we must accept them, whether we are attracted to the idea or not. In a real sense we are making a heaven now. Do you know the story of the man who arrived in heaven and was being shown around the 'many mansions' by Peter? They came to a rather dilapidated shack of which he was given the key. This was his heavenly 'mansion'. He was rather taken aback, and suggested that some mistake must have been made. But the apostle said, 'That is the best we could do with the material you sent up.' That is just a story but the idea behind it is soberingly true: the positive relationship between the bodily expression of our Christian lives, day by day, here and now, and the life that will be ours in the world that is to come (2 Corinthians 5:10).

Turn to Philippians 3:20-21. People ask us sometimes, 'Where do you stay?' The real answer to that is , 'Heaven.' We live here for a while, in various dwelling houses, but our citizenship is in heaven.

> 'But our commonwealth (literally our citizenship) is in heaven (our names are on the electoral register of the world that is to come), and from it we await the return of a Saviour, the Lord Jesus Christ, who will change our lowly body to be like His glorious body, by the power which enables Him even to subject all things to Himself.'

He shall change our bodies into the likeness of the body of His glory, and in this way we shall be fitted for glory and for service. Such a concept may be beyond our grasp, and this is understandable because here in this world we are, and always will be, limited. It calls for faith. But do we not feel some degree of thrill and anticipation? Once this limited lowly body of ours is changed, and all our ransomed nature in Christ Jesus is fitted with a body that 'does something for it', then we shall be able to serve Jesus and speak His praise in the way that we really want to.

Many Sundays a minister goes home thinking, 'It was

a glorious subject, but I wish I had been able to deal with it worthily.' Think of times when we are singing together in church, giving praise to God. Do we not sometimes feel the 'throb' of eternity and long to be all we should be for the Saviour's sake? With our resurrection bodies, free from all earthly limitation, and with coherent developed faculties and capacities, we will be able to serve well and worthily when we get to heaven. 'When we all get to heaven, what a day of rejoicing that will be.' All our disabilities and 'handicaps', physical, mental and emotional, will be gone.

The last passage for consideration is Mark 12:18-27. Here we begin to see how human thinking, too proud to know its limitations, ends up with a grotesque situation. It must have been a strange mind that thought up this conundrum for Jesus to answer. This is what happens when we are too proud to accept the fact that our limited intellect is incapable of grasping the whole spectrum of spiritual truth. This same grotesque form of thinking is evident when people speak in non-biblical ways of eternal things. A lady said, when her minister was talking to her about the salvation of her soul, 'I would rather be with my husband in hell than be in heaven without him.' But what right have we to assume that any given person will be 'ours' in hell? There can be no happy relationships in the dark place of judgment. This is wrong thinking. Jesus said it fails to grasp the Scriptures, or the power of God (Matthew 22:29).

We must not assume that everything in the world to come will partake of the same limitation and restriction as here upon earth. We must not project present conditions into the life that is to come. Granted, as we said in our previous studies, in the resurrection there is identity, which means we will know each other. We know each other here upon earth, and I doubt if we will be more stupid than that when we get to heaven! There is identity. There is continuity: the link between 'this' and 'that'. There is personality, as there is in the case of Jesus risen from the dead. 'Look', He says, 'It is I. I am your own Jesus' (cf. John 20:16-18). We will have bodies and bodily expressions of life and personality, but they will be quite transformed.

I used to have some difficulty about this, not so much when someone was buried in a grave, because that seemed at least to localise the mortal remains, but in the case of cremation, when the ashes may be scattered on the sea. But the resurrection of the body is not the gathering together of these particles, reconstituting them, and bringing them back to life. The two are connected but God gives a new body. Think of the illustration in 1 Corinthians 15:35 ff: the ripe full corn that grows out of the seed. Think of the daffodil with all its brilliant greens and yellows that grows out of the dull bulb, the oak tree that grows out of the acorn. Perhaps the best illustration of all is the butterfly with its brilliance of colour. (It is sad that with our insecticides we have killed off most of them.) Have you ever had a butterfly with all its wonder sitting on your finger? What brilliant artistry there is! That butterfly has come from the crawling caterpillar which withered and died, as it were, in its chrysalis, and ultimately it 'shuffled off this mortal coil', not without travail. Out of that withering and dying there comes the thing of beauty that is such a joy to see. The one body emerges from the other, but with a condition and an expression that is totally different.

Put it like this: it is the finite raised to share the infinite, without losing itself, without being absorbed. Have you ever been lost in a crowd? I can remember, as a child, being lost in a crowd. It was dreadful. In a great milling mass of people I was lost, and it did not appeal to me. Nor would it have appealed to me to be told that I had a real part in the great mass of humanity. I was not interested in the mass of humanity. I wanted to find my father. When we talk of the world to come, we are not talking about our souls being absorbed into the infinite or the eternal. I believe in 'the resurrection of the body and the life everlasting.'

I believe what Job believed:

> 'I know that my Redeemer liveth, and that He shall stand at the latter day upon the earth, and though after my skin worms destroy this body, yet in my flesh shall I see God' (Job 19:25-26 AV).

The moment that sight is mine, I shall know that this is only the beginning. But what a beginning! Freed from the limitations of a poor earthly body I shall become, in Christ, all that God has saved me to be, and I shall be able then in liberated personality through my new body to do what I shall never fully be able to do here upon earth. I shall be able to glorify God and enjoy Him for ever.

CHAPTER SIXTEEN

THE LIFE EVERLASTING

The closing phrase of the Apostles' Creed declares that we believe, 'in the life everlasting. Amen.' The final word is important. It indicates consent and affirmation rather than conclusion.

We deal with this final section of the Creed in terms of application based on all we have studied in the previous chapters. If we are honest we have to admit that the Bible is an embarrassing book. Compare its effect with the situation when a company of people are gathered for a social occasion. In the course of informal conversation one voice speaks up loudly introducing some subject that is bound to cause confusion and tension. In no time everybody begins to feel hot under the collar, and people try to cover up their confusion by changing the subject as quickly as possible. Evasion like this can arise when people are confronted with the questions raised by the Bible. Religion can be an embarrassing subject for many, but we must deal honestly with the Bible. We must allow ourselves to be cross-examined by some of the blunt, categorical, disturbing questions of Scripture.

It is easy to pride ourselves on our intellectual honesty and emotional stability. We Scots boast that we do not wear our hearts on our sleeves nor do we give way to emotion publicly, and we consider ourselves to be eminently practical in dealing with the business of life. But is it not true that we make a tremendous assumption as to the expectation of life, as did the man in the story in Luke 12:16-21? He calculated on five, ten, twenty years of life to come, and then suddenly his unrealistic intellectual reverie was broken into by a voice, which at first he did not fully understand, saying 'You fool, this night your soul is required of you.' I imagine that all of us assume we will get up and probably go to work tomorrow morning. But we have absolutely no right whatever to make that assumption. The man in the story made that assumption of life and he was wrong. The voice of God broke in upon his experience and told him his life on earth was over.

This man, in spite of all his intellectual capacity and careful business planning, was not allowed to build the extension to his barns. He was not allowed to finalise his financial accounts for the year. 'This very night', said God, 'your soul is required of you.' God did not mean later on that night, but right then, in the very speaking of the word, and the man found himself ushered out of time into eternity, out of this world into the world to come.

Think of him. Nothing of what he possessed was transferable to the world of eternity. He provided for his body, as is obvious from the story, and, if we assume he was a man who had family, I believe he provided also for his dependants. He was a man of some position in society, and I think it fairly safe to assume that he was a man of some public prominence in the business and commercial world. No doubt after his death and his funeral there would be a tombstone or a plaque unveiled in his memory, and his epitaph might possibly include a list of his public benefactions. But God's epitaph on this man is one word, 'Fool'. He had considerable capacity, but he was a man who throughout the whole of his life made no provision for the salvation of his soul. Perhaps he always meant to, but never got round to it. He never found the time to think of his soul, and then unexpectedly the time was gone.

Here is a man who failed to recognise or to live in the light of the world to come. The old hymn asks the question so pointedly, 'Where will you spend eternity?' This man failed to grasp the reality of eternity, the world to come, the unseen world, and we tend to be like him. Eternity is not far removed, some infinite distance away. It is through a very frail partition from the present life that we live in. It is a very flimsy partition, the thickness of one single breath. One moment you are breathing in time, the next you are in eternity. This man, with all his capacity, completely and utterly failed to make any preparation for the life that was to come. He forgot that he had a soul that needed to be saved. He wasted his time, and his time was gone. Little wonder you find urgency in the word of Scripture saying, 'Now is the accepted time, now is the day of salvation' (2 Corinthians 6:2 A.V.). Not tomorrow - today.

Notice carefully that there is absolutely no suggestion in the story of any obvious moral wrong or any sharp business practice in the whole of this man's life and activity. The blunder that he made was simply that he lived for the wrong world. When the world finished for him, and it finished far earlier than he expected, he was left with nothing. He had lived for the things that are seen and temporary, but the unseen and the eternal things of life had never been laid hold upon because of sheer neglect. I wonder if he ever went to church. I wonder if he had an evangelical minister. I wonder if he heard the gospel. I wonder if the Word of God at times pressed in upon him. But so preoccupied were his mind, his heart and his emotions with the things of time, of business plans and profits, that the things of eternity were forgotten, and through sheer neglect he lost his soul.

The embarrassing question we must face up to from this Scripture story is simply, 'Which world do we live for, this one, or the world to come?' What we call 'worldliness', a preoccupation with the things of this world has a debilitating effect on personality, and has had a tremendous effect on our whole generation of young people. We have rammed this world down their throats. We start speaking to them abut their careers, their prospects, and their retirement pensions, almost before they are out of primary school. By the time they are in their first year at work or university we are giving them pamphlets of information with regard to building society loans and credit cards which enable them to spend freely without reckoning on the 'pay-up' point. More and more we are anchoring them and ourselves into the fabric of a world that cannot last. We are providing for every possible contingency of earthly life, until there is scarcely an element of risk left in life. We are worldly-minded and we make our children the same by powerful conditioning from childhood on.

This is one of the reasons why many of the younger generation have become sick of and rebellious against the materialistic present and the nihilistic empty future of our social order. Many have begun to seek for life in and through experiences we call mystical and transcendental, as if some inarticulate part of their human personalities was saying that there must be more to life than this. They are right. Life is more than bread and circuses, pleasure and sensation. Ponder the verse in Ecclesiastes 3:11 which says that God has put eternity in man's mind. In the very constitution of human personality there is that eternal dimension which denies to mortal man rest or satisfaction of life until it is found in God Himself. Which life do you live for? Which world do you live for? This one or the one to come? Are you so preoccupied with this world that by sheer default and neglect you are in danger of losing your eternal soul? Turn to the Epistle of James 4:13,14:

'Come now (I think it could better be read, 'Now, just a minute'), you who say, "Today or tomorrow we will go into such and such a town and spend a year there and trade and get gain"; whereas you do not know about tomorrow. What is your life? For you are a mist that appears for a little time and then vanishes.'

The Book of Job (16:22) reminds us all:

'For when a few years have come I shall go the way whence I shall not return.'

Turn to Psalm 90 from which we get our hymn, 'O God, our help in ages past,' the hymn which goes on to say:

'Time, like an ever-rolling stream,
Bears all its sons away;
They fly forgotten, as a dream
Dies at the opening day' (Watts).

The Psalmist says:

'For a thousand years in Thy sight are but as yesterday when it is past, or as a watch in the night. Thou dost sweep men away; they are like a dream, like grass which is renewed in the morning: in the morning it flourishes and is renewed; in the evening it fades and withers' (90:4-6).

'For all our days pass away under Thy wrath, our years come to an end like a sigh, the years of our life are three-score and ten, or even by reason of strength, fourscore; yet their span is but toil and trouble; they are soon gone, and we fly away' (90:9-10).

'So teach us to number our days that we may get a heart of wisdom' (90:12).

Teach us to number our days, to count up the days that we have left. But we do not know their number.

Exactly! That is why it is so dangerous for some who know full well what it means to be converted to Christ to trifle and delay with that almighty decision they have yet to make for the salvation of their soul, and for their hope of heaven. God said to this man, 'You fool, this night........' This is not being dramatic or emotional, but realistic. Are your sins forgiven? Have you claimed Christ as Saviour? Is your soul in the safe-keeping of the only One who can bring you to God in peace and in blessedness?

The picture we are building up is one of men and women hurrying on into eternity. This man had made time to think about and prepare for every contingency except his soul's salvation. If you were going on a journey to London and you made provision for getting only halfway there, it would not be too serious because you could always make an adjustment. If you were making your journey to Australia and you made provision to get only as far as India that would be far more serious and less open to correction. If your journey was to be to the moon and you did not make sufficient provision to guarantee your safe arrival that would be stupidity in the extreme. Would you not say it was folly of a disastrous dimension to set out on a journey like that without providing for your safe arrival? What about the journey to eternity? We go hurrying on to eternity without making sure of that preparation and provision which concerns the salvation of our souls.

What is your life? The Bible speaks about the fleeting pleasures of sin (Hebrews 11:25). It also speaks of all that is in the world, the lust of the flesh, the lust of the eyes and the pride of life, and says that all of it passes away (1 John 2:16,17). Jesus says in the context of the story of the rich fool (Luke 12:15) that a man's life does not consist of the things that he possesses. That is not

195

life: that is just existence. Read, if you have the courage, the first three chapters in the Book of Ecclesiastes and you will find the account of a man of tremendous intellect, personality, and potential who set out to pursue fulfilment and ended up with nothing. I had cause some time ago to study these chapters very carefully and I found that that man, an attractive character in many ways, gave himself to wisdom and to the arts, to follow after madness and folly, to abundance of laughter and pleasure. He went on to give himself to the folly of wine. He was a man who tried to immerse himself in work, in gold, in music, in singing. He was the kind of man (and he had the capacity to do it) who said, 'Whatever my eyes desired I did not keep from them'(2:10). But in the end he said, 'Vanity of vanities,all is vanity' (12:8). He failed to find life. He did everything that this world gave him the opportunity to do, but there is no eternal life in anything that this world can give.

Jesus said: 'I came that they may have life, and have it abundantly' (John 10:10).

In what sense does Jesus bring life? He comes to us on the basis of His death and resurrection, to lift us up out of a mere human existence and bring us to life, separating us from our sins, so that all that is contrary to God in our lives is washed away by the merit of His dying love. Having brought us to forgiveness, He renews us by the Holy Spirit so that we are born again, born of God, with life that is not earthly but heavenly and eternal. Being born of the Spirit of God we become partakers of the divine nature, partakers of the very life of the eternal God Himself (2 Peter 1:4), here and now. This is life that is eternal, life that cannot be taken from us, life that cannot be corrupted, cannot be destroyed. It is ours in Christ and by Christ. It is life on a new dimension, above all that is merely worldly, with direction, purpose, and dynamic. The very power by which God raised Jesus Christ from the dead is the driving motive force of the life of every man and woman who has come to Jesus Christ. That is eternal life, and it begins now!

This life is found in one place and one place only, Jesus said:

> 'I am the way, the truth, and the life' (John 14:6).
> 'This is eternal life, that they know Thee the only true God, and Jesus Christ, whom Thou has sent' (John 17:3).
> 'This is the testimony, that God gave us eternal life, and this life is in His Son. He who has the Son has life; he who has not the Son of God has not life' (1 John 5:11,12).

What is your life? You could be like the man in the story, who knew all about these things but never took them seriously enough to compel him to make it all his own by opening his heart to Jesus Christ.

What about the last word? The life everlasting is offered to us in Christ, to be received by faith. What do we say to this? We say, 'Amen'. What does that mean? It means, 'Yes, God, that is for me'. A man called De Witt Talmage, a man mightily used of God in a past generation, preached a sermon on this fool and he ended by saying to the congregation, 'Bow your hearts, and put your heads down and speak your prayer to God here and now and tell Him that you come to Christ.' Then he looked up into the heavens and said, 'Oh, God, I've done my best to tell them to come. Constrain them by Thy Spirit, and bring them this very night to Jesus.'

What do you say to God?

> 'Just as I am, without one plea,
> But that Thy blood was shed for me,
> And that Thou bidd'st me come to Thee,
> O Lamb of God, I come' (Elliott).

Grant this to be the prayer of our every heart, O God, for Jesus' sake. Amen.

Books

available from

Christian Focus Publications

Geanies House

Fearn, Ross-shire

write for our current catalogue

There is
an Answer

Leith Samuel

Christians face problems

They need answers

God has the answer.

Leith Samuel, a well-known Bible teacher, gives spiritual advice on how to find the answer.

128pp   *pocket paperback*

Christian Warfare And Armour

by
James Philip

An exposition of Paul's description of the conflict between believers and Satan.

An exhortation to stand fast in the Lord.

An encouragement to fight until the victory is won.

James Philip is minister of Holyrood Abbey Church of Scotland, Edinburgh.

113pp   *pocket paperback*

Bible
Guidelines
by
Derek Prime

Teachings from the Bible

about
The Ten Commandments

The Fruit of the Spirit

Commitment to Christ

and

other areas of vital importance

Useful for personal or group Bible study.

Derek Prime is a well-known conference speaker and author

224 pages   *pocket paperback*